MARK ZWEIG & ASSOCIATES

More
Management
Ideas
That Work!

- in consulting engineering
- architecture &
- environmental consulting firms

by Mark C. Zweig

Another volume of
good ideas collected
from the best of
The Zweig Letter...

MARK ZWEIG & ASSOCIATES, INC.
NATICK, MASSACHUSETTS
SAN FRANCISCO, CA

Much of this book's content previously appeared in the periodical *The Zweig Letter* (ISSN 1068-1310)– Mark C. Zweig, Publisher; Frederick D. White, Editor; © Copyright 1992, 1993, 1994 Mark Zweig & Associates, Inc.

ISBN 1-885002-05-X

Also available from Mark Zweig & Associates, Inc.:

- MANAGEMENT IDEAS THAT WORK! (VOL. 1) (1993, $39)
- INSIDER'S GUIDE TO SF254/255 PREPARATION (1993, $79)
- INSIDER'S GUIDE TO CASHING IN ON YOUR EQUITY (1993, $79)
- INSIDER'S GUIDE TO GETTING INTO PRINT (1994, $79)
- VALUATION SURVEY OF A/E/P & ENVIRONMENTAL CONSULTING FIRMS (1995, $225)
- POLICIES & PROCEDURES SURVEY OF A/E/P & ENVIRONMENTAL CONSULTING FIRMS (1995, $195)
- MARKETING SURVEY OF A/E/P & ENVIRONMENTAL CONSULTING FIRMS (1994, $225)
- PRINCIPAL'S SURVEY OF A/E/P & ENVIRONMENTAL CONSULTING FIRMS (1994, $195)
- FINANCIAL PERFORMANCE SURVEY OF ENVIRONMENTAL CONSULTING FIRMS (1994, $225)
- SATELLITE OFFICE SURVEY OF A/E/P & ENVIRONMENTAL CONSULTING FIRMS (1994, $195)
- HUMAN RESOURCES MANAGEMENT: THE COMPLETE GUIDEBOOK FOR DESIGN FIRMS (1991, $60)
- THE ZWEIG LETTER (WEEKLY MANAGEMENT NEWSLETTER, $225/yr)

MARK ZWEIG & ASSOCIATES, INC.
ONE APPLE HILL, BOX 8325
NATICK, MASSACHUSETTS 01760
TEL (508)651-1559
FAX (508)653-6522

Contents

Preface

MANAGEMENT IDEAS THAT WORK! is back with more insights and information for design and environmental consulting firms.

As did its predecessor, *More Management Ideas that Work!* makes available a collection of practical and useful ideas and concepts that, if diligently implemented, will result in real success for your architecture, consulting engineering, or environmental consulting firm.

This book is just one of many publications from Mark Zweig & Associates that focuses solely on the needs of design and environmental firms. In fact, it is in this area where we concentrate our specialized management consulting practice, and we have succeeded by making firms like yours flourish. We're not the fly-by-night consultants who give it to you on paper and run. We have made our living by following the process right through the critical implementation stage...we stick it out and get real, measurable *results.*

We have extracted the finest articles from *The Zweig Letter* to create this helpful companion that highlights innovative solutions to the problems that can impede your firm's progress. You can start at any chapter you like, but we suggest reading it from cover to cover at least once. The arrangement of the chapters is alphabetical and there is a thorough table of contents in front and an index in the back to help you further isolate some problem areas.

This book is *not* a list of magical formulas, but it *is* a source of fresh and novel viewpoints that can help in addressing challenging issues. If you are a principal interested in getting the most out of your resources, embrace the advice contained in these pages, employ the management ideas that we have put forth, and experience greater success.

There still remains an endless sea of information on the inexact science of management for architecture, consulting engineering and environmental consulting firms. We can't possibly know it all, but we'll continue to chip away. Thankfully, there is a long road ahead of us. Success cannot exist without challenges.

In conclusion, I'd like to thank Jerry Guerra, associate editor of *The Zweig Letter*, for his invaluable input into the content and organization of this book.

I hope that you enjoy and benefit from reading *More Management Ideas That Work!* Please let us know your viewpoints and opinions...we would appreciate hearing from you. And if you know of someone else in your firm who could benefit from a copy, just contact us and we'll get one in his or her hands the same day. Dive in, learn, and enjoy!

Mark C. Zweig, President
Mark Zweig & Associates

December 1994

All about competitors

AS SOMEONE with a business orientation and education who started competing at a young age, I've always been interested in competition. I take pride in being a pretty competitive guy— one who likes to win whenever he can.

But as architects, engineers, and environmental scientists, the whole concept of competition may be foreign to you. You'll probably admit that you do have competitors— but for most of you, the people you square off against regularly are your former schoolmates, neighbors, fellow Rotarians, or someone you have commonality with through either your religion or your kids. As a result, these "peer-competitors" are certainly not— in *most* cases— anyone you would want to see *suffer*.

Let's look at some of the issues surrounding the subject of "competition," and how they could be affecting your firm:

People love to spread bad news. One thing's for sure— just about all intelligent people are critical, and they will inevitably gossip and say *bad* things about one another. It's human nature. Competitors are often the target of such discussion. After all, if you can't say something bad about a competitor, who can you say something *bad* about?

The "bad" news may be wrong. Because people love to spread a bad word, a lot of what you hear about your competitors probably isn't true. This was recently driven home to us. A 23-year-old civil engineer told us he wouldn't work for a particular firm in his area because he thought the firm was unethical. He said something had happened five or six years ago that he considered a conflict of interest. We knew his understanding of the event was hogwash, but he accepted what he heard from co-workers as the truth and *never* considered that his source could have been biased.

Successful firms make a great target. Just as with successful people, a successful *firm* probably has enemies. There will always be someone jealous of its success— someone who will try to take advantage of any misstep it might make in a project or business dealing. And my experience has been that if there isn't any dirt to dig up on the successful firm, someone will *make* it up.

Some people are just paranoid. I once worked for a guy who routinely *overestimated* how successful our competitors were. He would turn a five-person company into a 25-person company. I don't think he did it intentionally— it was just his nature to be fearful of anyone he thought could threaten us. But there are some firm leaders out there who deliberately whip their people into a frenzy about the competition to keep them from getting complacent.

Former employees make the toughest competitors. Occasionally, you'll meet someone in this business who is unusually focused on beating *one and only one* firm. My experience is that most of these people worked at that firm at one time. These former employees— whether they were fired or left the company on their own— have something to show the world. They may become obsessed with proving how *stupid* their former employers were for letting them get away. This gives them a focus and drive that sustains them through any obstacle, and makes them almost impossible to beat. And knowing the weaknesses of their competitor from the inside out only serves to fuel their fire.

Intelligence on competitors isn't that hard to get. Getting information on a competitor is pretty easy. I had one firm tell me how another company was trying to get access to their work product performed for a public sector client through the Freedom of Information Act. D&B financial profiles are available *instantly* through many on-line information services, and they can be very telling. Former employees of a firm may have a direct pipeline to that company's grapevine. State agencies' proposal files can tell you everything from billing rates to who a firm's best technical people are.

Like mosquitoes in the summer, competition in the A/E/P and environmental consulting business will *always* be there. But *good* competitors push us all to keep improving in every way. And although I hate to admit it, that's probably a *good* thing! ∎

D E T A I L S

WHERE TO GET information on your competitors:

Most A/E/P and environmental firms know very little about their competition. As a result, they are often ill-equipped to go head-to-head with their competitors in a tough battle to win a job.

There are many resources that are available to a firm that wants to know more about its competitors. Some of these include:

1. *Dun & Bradstreet (D&B).* Even if you're not a subscriber, there's nothing stopping you from running a D&B credit report on a competitor through one of the on-line services that carries D&B. It'll probably cost you $50 or $60, which isn't much when you consider what a great source of information it is. A D&B report can tell you a whole lot about how well your competitors are doing, who their principals and officers are, etc.

2. *Former/current employees of the firm.* Employees of your firm who used to work for a competitor are a great source of information. Take them out to lunch and ask some questions. Ditto for the employment candidates you might be interviewing from one of your competitors. They'll tell you a lot if you aren't afraid to ask.

3. *Clients.* Ask your clients what's good and bad about the other firms they deal with now, or have worked with in the past. Who are their best people? What are their strengths and weaknesses? Why does the client work/not work with the firm? What does the client like about do-ing business with their firm? What's not so great about their company?

4. *Public information sources.* We once sent an employee in our San Francisco office to Sacramento, where she spent the day photocopying engineering firm proposal files for a client. This was done with Caltrans' permission. As a result of the trip, our client knew *everything* about the other firms that were working for or trying to work for Caltrans, which included having full backgrounds on all of their people.

5. *Client perception surveys.* Use an outside contractor to conduct a client perception survey for your firm. The consultant will make a lot of phone calls and/or send out questionnaires to your clients and potential clients. In the process, undoubtedly they'll gather up useful intelligence on your competitors, which could be of use to you later on. Instruct the firm doing the client perception to probe their interviewees about the competition, especially any particular firms that you are interested in.

There are many, many sources of information on competitors. Use them all and you'll learn a great deal that could help you. But make sure to save this information in such a way that you can access it when you need it. Don't forget to allocate some file drawer space or computer storage to the material you've gathered up.

■

Are we like the "Big 6"?

ONE DAY not long ago, my co-workers and I found ourselves talking about the "Big 6" accounting firms and their problems. One of our newest staffers had just joined us from a Big 6 firm, and, believe me— those companies have *problems*.

I believe the Big 6 firms are doomed. We never cared much for them in the design industry— they certainly don't seem to do much business with any but the largest A/E or environmental consulting firms, and even then, only to the extent of audits or tax return preparation.

Why is that? Certainly one reason is the Big 6 accounting firms' billing rates seem astronomical to the typical engineering or architectural firm principal (who also sells his or her time for a living). Another reason is that most engineers and architects are wise to the benefits of specialization. They are selling their specialized knowledge and expertise to their clients every day. Why should they do business with a high overhead, non-specialized Big 6 accountant when there are so many other alternatives?

The woes of the Big 6 firms have some interesting parallels to the problems of the big, generalist A/E and environmental consulting firms. Yet, I talk with principals in design firms almost every day who are hell-bent on going down the same path as the Big 6 firms. What lessons can A/E and environmental consulting firms learn from the mistakes of Big 6 accountants?

1. **Big 6 accounting firms are filled to the brim with unproductive, disconnected principals.** A/E, consulting engineering and environmental consulting firms do not have a monopoly on dead weight. Just like the largest, do-everything-for-everyone A/E and environmental consulting firms, the biggest accounting houses are laden with top management that isn't selling, isn't doing, and isn't managing, yet continues to search for a job number they can charge some time against so they don't look too bad to their peers on management reports.

2. **Big 6 accounting firms are, just as their name implies, big.** They have lots of glitzy marketing materials, support staff of all kinds, a huge network of fancy offices in prestigious locations, incredible computer systems, and all of the resulting overhead. Just like the largest A/E and environmental firms, size does not necessarily equate with quality. Sometimes I think all it leads to is more disconnected employees who feel no passion for their work, their clients, or their firm. All this overhead is what makes the Big 6 firms so *expensive*, especially when you consider what the client is really getting.

3. **Because they aren't specialized, Big 6 accountants turn out "cookbook" products.** I'm constantly harping on how a lack of specialization impacts marketing. But more important is how it impacts *service*. Professional service firms that aren't specialized give no unique insight to their clients, chiefly because they have no unique insight to offer. And these generalists follow a cookbook that may not be applicable to the situation at hand. Anyone who has ever worked in the building design end of the business knows of a firm that designs every building the same. Whether it's a hospital, school, or hotel, they all look like they came out of one single factory.

4. **Generalist firms like Big 6 accountants are inherently *less efficient* than specialist firms**. In reality, generalists have to learn how to do each new job as they go along. They haven't developed a standard operating procedure for how the job will be accomplished, and if they have, it's probably wrong. Because of this, their quality is erratic, and they systematically become less and less profitable over time as they lose more and more focus.

5. **Big, generalist firms are less likely to rewrite the rules and innovate.** Like most big companies that have been around a while, Big 6 accounting firms have a lot to lose. So do the people working in them. The typical partner makes a tidy living and has significant value in his or her equity. As a result, these people (and those who aspire to be one of them some day) are not inclined to take risks or innovate, either in client service or internal management duties. The same thing is happening in the largest A/E and environmental consulting firms.

Just as I have come out strongly in favor of the benefits of focus and specialization, I have also always believed in the old adage: "Stop, look, listen, and learn." Sometimes, we need to stop for a moment, look beyond our own little world in the A/E and environmental consulting industry, listen to those in other similar worlds, and see what we can learn from them. **Z**

D   E   T   A   I   L   S

HOW DO you deal with an unproductive principal?

"It's one of those things they don't teach you in engineering school," says Mike Salmon, president of Salmon & Associates (Baton Rouge, LA), a 180-person consulting engineering firm. "They teach you all the technical things, but not about the people problems."

Here are suggestions for tackling this problem, before and after the fact.

Contractual provisions. This means a well written, legally enforceable buy-sell agreement. Dick Fruth, general manager of Hayes Large Architects (Altoona, PA), a 105-person A/E firm, says that firm's ownership contract has an exclusion clause. If a principal is dragging the firm down, the others can vote to buy that principal out.

Reassign the principal. Marty Dirks, president of KCM, Inc. (Seattle, WA), a 150-person E/A firm, has done several peer reviews for ACEC member firms. He recalls a situation when a talented principal was assigned work that did not challenge him. The principal's performance slumped. "They were just letting him drift," says Dirks. "When they moved him into a more important role, he excelled."

At a 160-person consulting engineering firm (that requested anonymity), a principal experiencing health problems was struggling at work. Everyone agreed to decrease his responsibilities and cut his work week to four days. They also reduced his salary and chances for advancement and additional income. The decision satisfied both sides, says the firm's president.

Reorganize. Another review by Dirks found two warring principals so caught up in their battle, neither was effective. Both reported to an absentee owner and were equals. The conflict actually revealed a fundamental problem in the organizational structure. The firm reorganized, giving each principal specific responsibilities that didn't overlap.

Get an outside opinion. An objective observer might help identify and correct a problem. "If our young guys here wanted to correct me, I'd suggest they hire a peer reviewer and have him tell me what a jerk I was," Dirks says.

Part ways. Dirks recalls a principal whose recent heart attack affected his mind, which hurt his work. "The firm wasn't doing well enough to get him out of there," says Dirks. "I recommended they borrow the money and buy him out. It was a good decision."

Salmon says shareholders and owners have to be open and try to help people who have drifted. But if they can't, they have to act. "When you know it's not going to work out, everyone has to realize the business is more important than any one individual."

■

Avoiding negotiation

CLIENTS OFTEN ASK if we do seminars on negotiating, what my philosophy is on negotiating, and what advice I have on negotiating. Architects, engineers, and environmental consultants can't seem to get enough on this topic because many of them spend a great deal of their time (*too* much, in my estimation) negotiating with clients.

Sure, I've read books written by the negotiation "experts," but their advice all seems to share one common element— *manipulation*. No matter how much everyone says a negotiation should be a win-win situation, most of what I have seen written is a thinly disguised attempt to help the reader *beat* the other guy through just about any means. And that usually mandates manipulation of one sort or another.

I don't like to negotiate. For the most part, our firm has been able to avoid it. How? First, we quote reasonable fees. Then, if a client doesn't want to work with us on the basis we propose, we've pretty much decided we're better off not working with them.

When firms do get into drawn-out negotiations with a client, it's usually because of one or more of the following:

1. Your client is someone whose *job* is to negotiate with you.

2. Your client doesn't *know* what he or she really needs.

3. Your client doesn't *want* to give you what you deserve.

4. Your client is reasonable, but *you* want too much.

Let's take a look at each of these situations in which you can get dragged into a negotiation:

Your client is someone whose job is to negotiate with you. If your client is a government bureaucrat or other paid negotiator who sees his or her entire job as getting the most out of consultants, whether you are being reasonable or not, there's not much you can do.

It's like taking a used car to a company that inspects cars for a living. They *will* find something wrong because that's what they are paid to do. Likewise, a paid negotiator will negotiate with you because that's what they are paid to do. The paid negotiator is not thinking about the long-term relationship you may have with the client and what that's really worth. Their role is to squeeze everything they can from you on this *one* contract.

Your client doesn't know what he or she really needs. In this case, *you* haven't done your job educating the client. Architects and engineers often assume all clients have the same full range of understanding they do— even non-technical clients or clients who are less experienced in the design and construction process. Before the negotiations start, it's your responsibility as a consultant to make sure the client has a complete understanding of the options available and has figured out what he or she really needs.

Your client doesn't want to give you what you deserve. This might be your fault or it might be your client's. You may not have made it clear how your services are different from those provided by your competitors. If that is the case, then keeping your fee down will be the primary thing driving your client. After all, the client figures he or she can get what you're providing from any number of sources— it's no slight against you, just rational thinking on the part of the client.

On the other hand, you may be dealing with a client that wants to rip you off. There are people out there who take pleasure in getting whatever they can out of anyone they do business with. Long-term relationships don't mean anything to them. Saving a nickel now is more important than saving a dollar later. These people secretly fancy themselves as predators entitled to prey on those lower in the food chain. If you get into negotiations with one of these clients, run— and don't look back! Whether it's now or later, you *will* end up with sour relations and some kind of dispute.

You want too much. If that's the case, shame on you! *You* are being greedy and deserve to have problems in your negotiation. Even if you do get the client to cave in to your demands, it will jeopardize your long-term relationship.

If you have done your homework in identifying the client's real needs, communicated what differentiates you from your competitors, and aren't overly greedy, you'll avoid a lot of time-consuming and profit-eroding negotiations and end up with clients that want to work with you again. **Z**

D E T A I L S

. . . .

IF DESPITE all your efforts to avoid negotiations with a client, you find yourself in a position where negotiating is unavoidable, you may want to take a look at some of the available literature on negotiations for the architecture, engineering, and environmental consulting industries.

The following titles were culled from the bookstore directories of the American Consulting Engineers Council (ACEC), the American Institute of Architects (AIA), and the American Society of Civil Engineers (ASCE). Please note that their listing here does not in any way imply the endorsement of Mark Zweig & Associates, Inc.

■ *The Architect's Handbook of Professional Practice.* A loose-leaf handbook that discusses many aspects of the practice of architecture. The "Projects" section covers initiating and acquiring projects, negotiating with clients, developing project agreements, and managing projects. (1994, AIA Press, 750 pages, $200. Available through the AIA Bookstore. Phone: 800/365-2724; Fax: 802/864-7626).

■ *Architecture: The Story of Practice.* A portrait of the architecture profession that discusses how design problems are construed and resolved, how clients and architects negotiate, and how design excellence is achieved. (1991, MIT Press, 320 pages, $15.95. Available through the AIA Bookstore. Phone: 800/365-2724; Fax: 802/864-7626).

■ *The Complete Negotiator.* Discusses how to develop a cooperative climate for a successful conclusion that makes everyone a winner. Includes strategies and tactics— determining your needs and those of the opponent. (1986, 345 pages, $24.95. Available through ACEC Bookstore: #926. Phone: 202/347-7474; Fax: 202/898-0068).

■ *Getting to Yes: Negotiating Agreement Without Giving In.* Step-by-step strategy for coming to mutually acceptable agreements in every sort of conflict. (1991, 200 pages, $22.95. Available through ACEC Bookstore: #1431. Phone: 202/347-7474; Fax: 202/898-0068).

■ *Negotiate Like the Pros.* ($9.95. Also available in video and audio cassettes. Available through ACEC Bookstore: #1158-C. Phone: 202/347-7474; Fax: 202/898-0068).

■ *Negotiation and Contract Management.* Based on the proceedings of a symposium sponsored by the Engineering Management Division of ASCE. The papers emphasize the importance of well negotiated and well written contracts. Topics include closed and silent negotiations, standard contract forms, and techniques of negotiation. (1985, ASCE, 50 pp., $15.00. Available through ASCE. Phone: 212/705-7242; Fax: 212/705-7300).

■ *Successful Negotiating for Engineering Services.* ACEC Audio cassette. ($10 for members/$20 for non-members. Available through ACEC Bookstore: #708. Phone: 202/347-7474; Fax: 202/898-0068).

■

Being a good boss

MANAGEMENT people are usually critical of technical people for their lack of business knowledge. But having a business degree is *no* assurance you know any more than the average design or environmental consultant about how to *supervise* people. They just don't teach you how to be a *supervisor* in school.

In fact, I saw an interesting article recently that said one's score on the GMAT (Graduate Management Aptitude Test), a test used to judge admittance for most MBA programs, was *inversely* related to actual ability to supervise people. Those with GMAT scores of 700 or higher— while they may perform *very* well in the typical overly quantitative MBA program— don't have the interpersonal and communication skills necessary to be a good boss.

Beyond the educational system's lack of an attempt to teach supervisory skills is the bad programming managers get— all too common in the typical A/E or environmental consulting firm. Being a "boss" is a big responsibility. Here's some of what I have learned over the years:

1. **Good selection is 80% of the game.** The fact is and always has been that if you get the right people in the first place, they will take very little time to manage. Yet, recruiting is usually way down the list in terms of its *real* priority to management.

2. **Give people enough rope to hang themselves, but first teach them how to make the noose.** It's one thing to let people go on their own, to learn from their own mistakes. We all learn better that way. But first you have to teach people how you want things done if you ever hope for them to be able to meet your expectations.

3. **Don't wait to deliver negative feedback.** Storing up your criticisms of an employee's behavior is potentially one of the most harmful things you can do. Being continuously critical may result in a perception of your staff that you are a nit-picker. But it also *reduces* the likelihood an explosive confrontation over some little issue— one that results in the company and the employee parting ways. I can't tell you how many times I have seen a normally calm architect or engineer who happens to be a manager *explode* at an employee— lashing out because of their own inability to be direct when they should have been.

4. **Do the same with your praise as you do with your criticism.** Show that you recognize when somebody does something good. If that's working a lot of hours, let them know that you know they are doing it. If it's putting extra quality into something, let them know you appreciate it.

5. **Be friends with your people.** There's *nothing* wrong with befriending an employee as long as you don't forget that you are also their boss. It helps if you don't act like you are infallible. Showing your vulnerability by admitting a mistake goes a long way to building up mutual trust, which is essential to good communication. It is only through real sharing that the employee can figure out what you want and you can figure out what the employee wants— essential ingredients to a long-term relationship of mutual benefit.

6. **It's worth trying to turn somebody around.** It's easy to be the hard guy and be dispassionate. I do it in turnaround situations regularly. But when the firm is *not* in a turnaround situation, I also realize that the cost of replac-

ing people is enormous. People *can* turn it around if you are straight with them. I have seen it over and over. On the other hand, readers need to understand my advice here. I do not advocate *ignoring* the problem and doing *nothing* about it. That's not a turnaround— that's wishful thinking.

7. **Be straight with people about what their likely career potential is with your firm.** Don't build unrealistic expectations. Unrealistic expectations lead to *unsatisfactory* employer-employee relationships. That is at the heart of most every parting, at either end. You have to tell people what is likely, so they can plan accordingly.

8. **Pay people what they are worth, not the least you have to in order to get them on board.** Being cheap is typical of the behavior negotiating experts advocate— get every nickel you can, but disguise it as "win-win." Let's stop kidding ourselves. Employees pay attention to what you do— not what you say. If you tell them you will reward them, you better reward them. And don't be afraid to give rewards quickly.

9. **If you want people to sell, react very carefully to the opportunities they bring in.** Boy, we have a problem with this one in the A/E and environmental consulting industry. We'll tell our people we want them to sell, then poo-poo whatever opportunities they find because they aren't "what the firm is all about," or because they are "too small," or because *we* didn't bring them in. Maybe you can't chase after something an employee thinks you should. But *how* you handle telling them makes all the difference in the world in whether they will bring in the next opportunity for you to consider.

This isn't academic theory. I know that anyone who uses these principles to guide their daily activities will be a better boss. **Z**

D E T A I L S
• • • • • • • • • • • • • • • •

THE 40-HOUR work week is a myth in consulting engineering, architecture and environmental firms. But how do you motivate salaried staff to work those profitable over-40 hours?

Paying overtime is usually *not* the answer. As we've written in the past, overtime for professionals is not a good idea because it becomes expected and is often abused.

Paul Grupe, executive vice president of Facility Engineers, Inc. (Smyrna, GA), a 75-person A/E firm, says people will fit whatever work they have to do into whatever block of hours they are permitted to use, even if they don't intend to.

"When I decided not to work on Saturday, I found out I was still getting the same amount of work done," says Grupe. "I was planning on the extra time, so I fit in some other activities I normally wouldn't have, like sitting around talking about the NCAA tournament."

Here are three suggestions for enticing salaried employees to put in more than 9-to-5. Note, they don't apply to hourly, non-exempt personnel:

Make it a job requirement. "In a couple of our offices, we have a mandatory 50-hour work week," says Lee Smith, chairman of Handex Environmental Recovery (Morganville, NJ), a 170-person environmental firm. "The guys that run the offices say, 'You're professionals and this is what we expect of you.'"

Smith says these professionals earn "incentive hours," as do other salaried and hourly personnel in the company. That system pays exempt workers a fixed rate, usually about $15-$17 an hour, for all *chargeable* hours above 35 a week, with a variable ceiling depending on the project and other factors. But their salary is based on 50 hours *worked* per week.

Pay people what they're worth. If you pay a competitive salary, your staff shouldn't be counting hours. Donald McEdwards, president of Trans Tech Consultants (Santa Rosa, CA), a 16-person environmental firm, says he is considering changing his system of paying overtime to his people who work more than a set number of hours (usually 40-44). "Many of them are compensated enough with their salary, vacations and other benefits," says McEdwards. "They should be expected to work whatever it takes to get the job done. That's what the salary is for at the higher levels."

Be generous with bonuses. An incentive compensation system based on company and group profitability, combined with occasional discretionary bonuses, is better than overtime for compensating extra effort. Why? First, because *management* gets to define the plan and control the rewards (with overtime, *employees* get to set and collect their bonuses on the "installment plan"). Second, unlike overtime, bonuses reward results, not just hours.

Better marketing

ECAUSE marketing really is "where it's at" for firms in this business, it's hard for me to keep from writing about it. You see, an A/E/P or environmental consulting firm can solve just about *any* problem, *if* marketing works like it's supposed to. If clients are beating down your door to hire your firm, there will probably be time to stave off creditors, attract the staff you need, solve operational problems, and make a profit.

Here are some suggestions for more effective marketing:

1. **Don't spend one nickel keeping firms off of your prospect list.** I find it fascinating so many A/E/P firms actually spend money to keep buyers and potential buyers off their marketing contact list. I'm talking about doing things like making it a requirement that no one can be added to the list unless someone in the firm has actually met that person; "pre-qualifying" clients by pulling out those we think won't have a budget for our services during the coming year; or eliminating potential clients who are already working with a capable competitor. None of this makes any sense. What we *should* do is try to get every single buyer, potential buyer, and influencer of the buying decision on our lists, and then bombard those people through every available means. Then when they call us, we can decide if we want to pursue each job or cli-

ent relationship on a case-by-case basis. The only potential clients I don't want on the list are criminals who don't pay their bills— they go on a different (i.e., "black") list.

2. **Don't make PR any tougher than it is.** Nothing is much easier for do-it-yourselfers than public relations. For most firms in this business, it's simply a numbers game. Send out enough press releases and eventually you'll find your name in print. Include some publications you might normally not, such as *The Wall Street Journal* or the airline magazines. What's realistic? You may only get one or two percent of your press releases picked up— that's two or four articles per 200 releases mailed. But that's OK. It only costs you $60 to $80 to send out 200 releases, if you make the copies yourself. There's no cheaper advertising!

3. **Capture every inquiry from a client or potential client.** Each person who calls your firm should be logged into your client database. These people would not be contacting your firm if they did not see you as a possible source for what they need— whether that's to help them solve a problem or capitalize on an opportunity. So why lose contact with them if you don't get together this time?

4. **Get all the work you can from local clients before you go out of your area to find new ones.** This helps keep marketing *and* operational costs down. I'm convinced some people in this business really *love* to travel, despite what they might say to the contrary. Why else would someone travel to Timbuktu at the drop of a hat to chase the most remote possibility of getting a job? Very few design or environmental firms have more than a single-digit percentage of the markets they are *now* in, and many have only a few tenths or even *hundredths* of a percent of their local market— yet their principals will go out of state (or out of the country) to find new prey.

5. **Go after fewer jobs, not more jobs.** About 85% of a firm's marketing resources are consumed reacting to opportuni-

ties that come in over the transom, usually in the form of an RFP or *CBD* announcement. But firms pursue so many, they don't have enough time or money to react properly to them all. It's not uncommon for a marketing manager or marketing coordinator to turn out 20, 30, or even 40 proposals each month! With that level of activity, is it any wonder the stuff they put out is 94% fat and only 6% beef?

6. **If you find one person with a problem, call everyone in that role in similar organizations, and you'll probably find that they have the same problem.** This idea was taught to me by my first post-graduate-school, work-world mentor. He said this is the fastest way to cash in on recently acquired experience. Look to existing clients' competitors or peers for more of what you are doing now.

7. **When it comes to building relationships, aim high.** One of the biggest mistakes marketers in this business make is that they enter the organization at too low of a level. There are certainly exceptions to this. But you'll almost always get more out of a relationship with the top person in a client organization than with someone at the bottom or middle. The top person can always *kick* you down, but it's a lot harder to get *pulled* up. **Z**

D E T A I L S

· · · · · · · · · · · · · · · · · · · ·

HOW DO you keep track of clients, contacts and prospects? A Rolodex? Scattered notes on napkins and matchbook covers? If so, or even if you're using an outdated computer system, you're not getting the most from the technology available.

"The computer age allows us to be more effective. With client contact software, I can instantly recall the last five conversations I've had with a client. I could never do that before," says Gary Hunt, managing partner of 310-person A/E firm Gresham, Smith & Partners (Nashville, TN).

Hunt's firm bought client contact software called *Gold Mine*, and principals and marketers use it on their office computers and laptops. It is a "stand-alone" product, meaning each user maintains his or her own database, and information is not networked to others in the system. But the firm keeps a central database at headquarters to keep track of every user's contact list.

Hunt says the firm spent $5,000-$7,000 for the program and 12 licenses, and another $250 for each additional license. "The software is relatively inexpensive," he says. "The major expense is the laptop computers to run it on."

The Durrant Group, Inc. (Denver, CO) is upgrading its client contact software and is leaning toward a product called *ACT*. Marlin Weikum, information systems manager for the 170-employee A/E firm, says of the product, "It can update the contact databases in several geographic areas through the E-mail program we have."

Groundwater Technology, Inc. (Norwood, MA), a 1,700-employee, multi-office environmental firm, uses a networked system from a company called *Marketing Information Systems.*

"We chose this one because it allowed a reasonable amount of custom tailoring," says John Henderson, marketing systems specialist. "They built the shell and we customized the parts unique to our business."

Henderson says the system has almost completely solved the problem of coordinating several different client contact lists from its 60 offices and 35 full-time sales people. The firm sent out 15,000 pieces in its first mailing using the new system in early 1992, and *34%* came back because the addressee had moved, retired, died or wasn't there for some other reason. In its most recent mailing, 17,000 pieces went out and only *2%* returned.

"We're finding companies are responding to our improved accuracy," says Henderson. "Our level of professionalism is going up and we're not wasting money on bad mail."

■

Better writing

SOME READERS might think that a discussion of writing has no place in a management publication aimed at architects, engineers, and scientists. They couldn't be further off the mark.

Good writing skills are absolutely *critical* to anyone who wants to be a success in the A/E/P or environmental consulting business. One of the greatest single complaints from top managers in this business is that professionals don't know how to write. The principals of a 70-person environmental firm recently told me that only six people had decent writing skills!

Most of what we do requires writing— proposals, letters, reports, memos, and so on— yet many technical people have had absolutely no formal training (or informal, for that matter) on how to write effectively. That's too bad, because writing is something that all of us can improve on. Unlike some other aspects of management, good writing skills *can* be taught. Here are some pointers that I have found helpful over the years— maybe you will, too:

1. **Avoid jargon, buzzwords, and cliches.** One of my biggest complaints with the writing samples that I review from people in this industry is that we get carried away with jargon and buzzwords, which may be familiar to us but aren't to the rest of the world. I mean phrases like

"change out the coil" or "introduce prestressing into the cables." We also tend to overuse the same old tired cliches like "state-of-the-art," "innovative," "cost effective," and so forth. The result is that we either intimidate, confuse, or bore the reader, who is often one of our clients (or potential clients).

2. **Keep sentences short and minimize multi-syllable words.** Why use "utilize" when "use" will do? Why have a 49-word sentence when three 15-word sentences could be used? I'm not sure I know *why* we do these things, but the fact is that we *do*. Maybe we think it makes us look smart. But it doesn't! Once again, the effect on the reader is boredom, intimidation, or both.

3. **Watch out for stilted language.** The reason we use stilted language, particularly in business letters, is that we all learned how to write them from our bosses. Our bosses learned from their bosses, and so on, going way back to the 19th century! When I talk about stilted language, I'm referring to terms such as "enclosed herewith" or "as per your request." *No one* talks like this conversationally, so why make your letters that way? The use of stilted language hurts your ability to communicate.

4. **Know what you want to say and make an outline before you start.** It's amazing how few writers actually do this. Before starting anything, I decide what I am trying to communicate. I make sure those things are addressed in my letter, report, memo, article, or whatever. I also use an outline. The term paper format taught me by my 10th grade American History teacher (the first teacher to give me a "D" on a paper) can be adapted to any type of writing. You start with an introduction that tells readers *what* you are going to tell them. Then in the next three paragraphs (or three pages, or three sections) you tell them what you said you would tell them. Then the conclusion tells them what you told them. Try the formula— it works!

5. **Cut, cut, cut.** It's easy to be long-winded; it's hard to be concise. But the effort is worth it. Revisit everything you write and omit needless words. Cut pointless paragraphs or sections. Eradicate all of the garbage. Then your message will shine through loud and clear, and you'll truly look smarter to the outside world.

6. **Don't always fall back on the last proposal, letter, or memo you wrote.** Sometimes you are much better off taking out a clean sheet of paper than you are going back to a similar document and using that as a starting point. That way, you won't tend to repeat the same mistakes over and over and over again. You'll also find that new ideas come to you more easily when not surrounded by a lot of old ones.

7. **Read what you wrote out loud.** Does it sound ridiculous? If so, change it.

The writing skills of the professionals working in this business are weak. At least that's what many top people in the industry think. That's why teaching your people to write could really separate *your* firm from the rest of the pack. **Z**

D E T A I L S

· · · · · · · · · · · · · · · · · · ·

WRITING RIGHT: Engineers at 185-person environmental consulting firm Whitman & Howard, Inc. (Wellesley, MA) are working to improve one of the profession's typically weak areas— writing. Mike Reilly, the company's communication manager, conducts a course to help teach the firm's technical professionals how to write better.

"Like a lot of firms, we realized a weakness was our technical staff's writing," says Reilly, who has conducted the course several times since 1991. "Instead of taking a grammatical or academic approach, we try to teach the tools of writing to engineers in formats they're familiar with. Letters, proposals, client reports. It's much easier for me as a trainer, and much more familiar for them."

The most difficult part of the course is teaching technical people to write for the layman, Reilly says. "I say, 'When you're done writing something, show it to your wife, your mother or your brother. If they can figure it out, then you've got it,'" he says.

The part of the course his trainees remember most is the "Gunning Fog Index," which helps judge the clarity of a piece by counting the number of letters per word, words per sentence and sentences per paragraph, and plugging it into a formula.

"Engineers love it because it's a formula," says Reilly. "The whole thing is getting them into clarity. When a reader is confronted with a lot of long sentences and multi-syllable words, it gets confusing."

Reilly says he sometimes has to convince his students that shorter can be better. "They think clients want a big, thick document because that's what they paid for," he says. "But people now just want to get to the point."

Reilly has presented the course to the Connecticut Society of Professional Engineers (Hamden, CT) and the Society for Marketing Professional Services (SMPS) (Alexandria, VA) Fundamentals Program. "It's easy because most of the participants realize this is a weak area for them," Reilly says. "They come really willing to listen."

■

WRITING HELP: *The Elements of Business Writing*, by Gary Blake and Robert W. Bly, has been around for a couple of years. It's the kind of book you're likely to find in the office of a corporate communications manager or marketing director, but if you do any writing related to your work— letters, memos, project proposals, etc.— it should be on a shelf in your office.

The beauty of this 140-page guide is its focus. It doesn't waste time on rules of grammar you couldn't understand or be bothered with in grade school. It offers simple, practical advice on ways you can improve the clarity and effectiveness of your business writing. The book is published by Macmillan Publishing Co. and is $9 in paperback.

■

Beyond "paper" qualifications

WHEN it's time to hire, most A/E and environmental consulting firms do a pretty good job defining their needs in terms of education, registrations, experience, and so forth. But they *don't* do a good job defining the "other" requirements for the person they need to hire.

No one bats a thousand, but many firms can improve their average *if* they approach recruitment and hiring from a different perspective. Here are some suggestions for reviewing job candidates that will increase your chances of picking a winner:

1. **Communications skills.** If someone can't even write a decent cover letter, how in the world will he or she be able to function effectively as a consulting engineer, architect, or environmental consultant? You've got to be able to write and speak well in this business to sell work, manage people, and put together a good deliverable.

2. **Appearance.** The human resources people may have a fit about this one, but let's face it— looks *are* important to success in this business. One of my clients once asked me where he could find a mechanical engineer who wears $70 ties— he didn't believe there *were* any! And appearance goes beyond dress— it goes to the quality of one's

briefcase, the condition of his or her car, and personal hygiene.

3. **Good grades.** All factors being equal, I would hire the person who made better grades in school. This is especially true for people who haven't been in the working world for too long. What other indicator of their performance do you have? There are all kinds of exceptions, but generally speaking, the "A" students may be a little bit smarter, a little more disciplined, and a little more performance-oriented than the "B" or "C" students.

4. **No obvious failures.** It would concern me if a job candidate couldn't pass the EIT exam, or had failed the P.E. test three times in a row, or worse, failed as marketing director in two separate companies. Why hire anyone who has a track record of failure if you can get someone who has been a success?

5. **Not too many jobs.** It always concerns me when I see a candidate who has had five jobs in the last 12 years. There may be all kinds of explanations for it, but the inability to last on a job more than a year or two is a tip-off that something is wrong.

6. **Done it before.** The probability of success in the job increases when the employee is a proven performer in a similar role. He or she will have more realistic expectations of the job, not to mention having learned something in the past that can be used in your firm.

7. **Not looking.** When I conduct staff interviews for a management audit, I usually ask each person how he or she came to work at the company. It tells me something if everyone responded to a newspaper ad rather than being recruited away from their previous employers. People who are *not* looking are a lower risk than those who are either unemployed or desperate to make a change so they can *escape* their present job. Those not looking will only make a change when it is smart to do so— they've got a good job at risk.

8. **Family background.** Again, it makes the H.R. people nervous, but I like to know the family background of anyone who will be functioning at a middle or upper level. Two types of people seem to be the most successful— those who come from a successful family where everyone is a high achiever, and those who come from a not-so-successful family that the candidate broke out of. When the person comes from a "success" background, he or she is more likely to live up to that expectation. When someone comes from a tough background, yet got through school and struggled to get ahead, hunger and fear of returning to his or her origins can be a strong motivator.

9. **Cultural fit.** This is made up of a wide variety of factors— including personality, age, educational background, and where someone grew up. You *can't* illegally discriminate and you *don't* need everyone to be the same, but you can't overlook how someone will fit in. I think back on one 55-year-old Texan who went to work for a predominantly Asian firm in a very liberal part of the country— he didn't last. It reduces risk when you hire people from the local area.

10. **Strong work ethic.** Give me someone who works 60 hours a week over someone who thinks they can do it in 40. One of my more successful clients calls that "the extra hour advantage." There really isn't any substitute for hard work. And just because someone doesn't have billable work to do doesn't mean there's no need to work extra hours. That's the time to develop standards, get organized, and *sell.* **Z**

D E T A I L S

· ·

TWO READERS disagreed with parts of our editorial, "Beyond 'paper' qualifications," which advised principals not to overlook the intangible factors when hiring managers.

Mary K. Van Domelen, CFO at BOORA Architects, P.C. (Portland, OR), writes, "The work force in the architecture and engineering professions continues to evolve into one of greater variety and diversity. Smart, forward-looking A/E firms are embracing this evolutionary change and realizing that unity of purpose and commitment does not come from sameness— it comes from a shared vision coupled with mutual respect for differences. Also, a firm's strength is owed in great part to a commitment by top management to hold diversity as a core value."

Alfred Chock, senior engineer at a Boston-area firm (who asked that his firm name not be used), objects more strongly. "I notice that none of the intangibles you list provide insight into a candidate's integrity, honesty, and sense of ethics. Clients seek these qualities when establishing long-term relationships. They are far more valuable than $70 neckties.

"I believe you have confused the cultural background of an individual employee with the corporate culture of a company. That mistake is unworthy of a newsletter that purports to teach others how to manage their businesses. The only 'cultural fit' worth striving for is that between the individual and the corporate culture."

We thought that's what we were saying— consider how someone will fit into the corporate culture. That doesn't mean a 42-year-old Italian-American from the Midwest should stock his firm with people who are exactly the same. And it certainly doesn't mean exclude anyone because of color, age, national origin, or religion.

The issue is sensitive. As the article said: "You can't illegally discriminate and you don't need everyone to be the same; but you can't overlook how someone will fit in."

■

LIKE MOST of you, we receive many résumés a week. Once in a while, we get some truly entertaining submittals, and over the years, we've filed them in a folder marked "Award-winning résumés":

■ A candidate for a marketing director position sent, along with his résumé, a psychological profile report that included a section headed, "Attitudes About Sex." The text described the candidate's style of lovemaking in rather lurid detail.

■ An engineering résumé listed as hobbies "whistling, collecting rocks." Another listed "sculpting clay kittens."

■ An environmental engineer and scientist seeking a management position needed half a page to detail his educational training: three PhD's, four Master's degrees, and two undergraduate degrees.

■

Brag, brag, brag...

As Art Linkletter observed: "Kids say the darnedest things." One day, my daughter Christina, who was at the time in the first grade, said to me, "Dad, why don't you do a commercial where you tell everyone how great you are and how perfect your company is?"

"Well, Christy," I said. "When you see those commercials on T.V., or read ads like that in a magazine, does it make you want to buy what they are selling?"

"No," she said "It just sounds like they're *bragging.*"

"You just answered your own question," I said.

She then asked me: "How do you sell your books and other jobs, then?"

"By giving people information about the product or service, or by giving people some other information they want or need so they can see we understand their business," I told her. "Then they call us."

The very next day, a brochure from an engineering firm in the Midwest hit my in-box. I opened it up, and here's what I read (with the names changed to protect the innocent):

"From its beginning in 1935, with John Jones and a staff of three men, the firm has greatly expanded its staff... The widely varied projects turned out during the past years have been of particular importance to our clients. With this background of successful engineering services, it is of paramount importance

that continuing reasonable solutions to engineering problems be achieved."

I wasn't sure what I read, but I knew that they wanted me to think they were good. Out of curiosity, I pulled out some more brochures from other, larger firms, just to see what they were saying. One large engineering firm's brochure starts out:

"Across America and around the world, the firm of XYZ Associates is known as one of the leading American _____ engineers in the design of _____."

Don't laugh. It continued:

"Headquartered in _____ for nearly 30 years, XYZ Associates has been recognized internationally with hundreds of awards for innovative designs of state-of-the-art _____s and _____s."

I'm sure they must be proud. The next brochure stated:

"As we review our performance, a look back at just a few of our landmark projects is doubly rewarding. It reminds us of where we have been, as a firm and as individuals, earlier in our careers."

I'm glad they are pleased with themselves. Then I pulled out another brochure that read:

"ABC Associates, founded in 1953, boasts a management team which brings together many years of experience in the consulting engineering, architectural, and management fields." They went on to say, *"For numerous years, ABC's record of service has brought us repeat business from our loyal clients."*

They weren't kidding when they said *boast!* The next brochure I read opened up with:

"John Public & Associates, Inc., successfully conducts complete architectural and engineering programs, culminating in aesthetically and functionally pleasing products. Exciting results are achieved through carefully tailored and managed programs, that build from initial client parameter meetings through creative concepts, planning, budgeting, design and production stages." Whew— that was a mouthful! I dug into my file cabinet even deeper for yet another brochure from a mid-sized, multi-discipline firm and just skimmed the headlines, which promised *"Innovative Yet Practical and Cost Effective Solu-*

tions" plus *"Multi-Disciplinary Service," "Highly Qualified Staff,"* and *"Ever-Changing Services."*

My reaction to all of this stuff: Is this what consulting engineers and architects really think makes people want to buy their services? Can't they recognize tired cliches? Can't they see that none of this communicates *any* degree of understanding for their clients' business? It's just bragging.

Why not try this exercise with your own firm's literature? It's time to go back and look at your brochures and marketing materials. Let's be careful not to insult the intelligence of those who read these things. Even a first grader can tell you that bragging turns people off. **Z**

D E T A I L S

IT SEEMS LIKE every time I look in my in-box, I see a conference brochure, seminar flier, newsletter, or magazine article that looks like the author got paid based on how many multi-syllabic buzzwords (or as I like to call them, "buzzterms") he or she could use.

What is it about the buzzterms that seem to fascinate some people in our business? "Paradigm Shift," "Megatrends," "Re-engineering," "Customer Focused Enterprise," "Workplace Integration," and so on are all becoming more commonplace in the management literature for the A/E and environmental business than honest, meat-and-potatoes words like "client," "design," "service," "marketing," and "recruiting."

I'm convinced the people who routinely drop these terms do so for one of two reasons: Either a) They're incapable of an original thought, and are therefore perpetuating somebody else's thinking; or b) They're insecure in their business capabilities and it makes them feel good about themselves to intimidate technical people who don't have any business education.

You won't hear those buzzwords in *The Zweig Letter* unless we are poking fun at them. That's because we don't read every new business book written and then regurgitate it with a periodic reference to A/E/P and environmental firms. That's not our formula and it never will be.

We base our writing on our own experience and that of the 50,000 A/E/P and environmental firms that make up this incredibly diverse in-

dustry of ours— not that of disconnected academic, self-employed (or unemployed) "consultants," or people from some business completely unrelated to yours and ours.

■

BROCHURE POINTERS:

Don't mass mail your brochure. If you do, probably the only people you'll hear from are your competitors who will call and say, "Nice Brochure, Bob. Who did that for you? We've been trying to get ours updated for the past three years but just can't seem to get it done."

Don't let your technical/professional staff convince you they can't sell without a brochure. That's just an excuse for their own lack of interest in selling. Remember that a brochure is a "defensive" piece of marketing literature. Brochures are not a substitute for a sales call— they *support* a sales call.

Design a piece that won't go out of date. How will you update the address and phone number, or add/change branch office locations if necessary? Look at the people in your photos, their hair styles and how they are dressed. Is there anything in the brochure that could make you look ridiculous?

Make up separate brochures for your satellite offices. Constantly fighting the image of being out-of-towners, the last thing branch offices want to see is a brochure with a huge "Corporate Headquarters in Topeka" on it when they are in Cedar Rapids.

■

Burdens of being a boss

ALMOST every motivated person in an A/E/P or environmental consulting firm is either already a manager, or wants to be one. That's OK, but not all of these people really understand what it means to take on that responsibility. And as principals, we usually don't prepare them for it very well.

Here are my thoughts on what a design or environmental firm professional needs to do to become a successful *boss*:

1. **You have to set the right example.** If you want your people to work a lot of hours, *you* have to. If you want them to produce perfect documents, *you* have to. If you want them to always have a contract with a notice-to-proceed in-hand before starting work, *you* have to operate that way. If you want them to live frugally while on the road, you have to live frugally. You will be judged by your staff in this manner, and there's no way you can change that fact.

2. **You have to lead fearlessly.** If a client is taking advantage of your firm, you have to assert yourself. If a client is getting ready to make a big mistake, you have to tell them so and explain why. If your boss has a misconception about one of your people, you have to stand up for

him or her. As a manager, your people will look to see how fearless you are before they line up behind you.

3. **You have to create work for *others* first.** Architects, engineers, and scientists all have a problem with this one. Too many think that if they are billable themselves, that's all that counts. That may be true if you *aren't* a manager, but the day you become one, it's how you *feed* the people who work for you that counts. Any good professional can get enough work to support him- or herself, but *managers* have to take care of others first.

4. **You have to be an optimist.** No intelligent person wants to work for someone who is negative or a defeatist. It's no fun. Managers have to project the confidence that the team will overcome all obstacles and emerge victorious in the end. If you are a manager and you constantly complain about the firm's principals, your clients, the economy, the marketplace, or whatever, *no one* will want to work for you.

5. **You have to be fair.** When you become a boss, a certain amount of power automatically comes with the position. And how you use this power is really where the rubber meets the road. Every team will have some people in it that you like better than others. As a manager, you'll start getting control over how at least *some* (if not all) of the goodies are given out— whether that means pay increases, verbal praise, spot bonuses, or better project assignments. But just because you are the boss, you can't give all the gravy to the people you *like* the best. You have to consider who deserves a pat on the back or a serious blasting. You have to keep *everyone* on your team happy and moving in the right direction, and that requires being fair.

6. **You have to put the team first.** This must come before any individual's needs— especially *your own*. Is it right to pick out a new Infiniti for your company car— even if you are personally picking up the tab for the difference in the

lease payment between that and a Park Avenue Ultra—and to then tell your people there won't be any pay increases this year? Is it right to order new office furniture for yourself, then make one of your lower level staffers sit in a chair with a back that is falling off? Should *you* have a Pentium machine on your desk that is only used for word processing, when one of your key professionals is doing seismic analysis computations on a vintage IBM AT? Should you be the only one who gets a bonus when the rest of your group gets nothing? The answer to all of these questions is probably "no."

7. **You have to admit your mistakes.** If you think you can't make a mistake, because you are the boss and you are supposed to be better than anyone else, you have a warped view. You always get more mileage by being completely open about your mistakes than you *ever* do by trying to pin them on someone else. Managers must assume responsibility for what they and their staff do— that's how they build allegiance.

8. **You have to avoid the temptation to remind your people that you are the boss.** A woman I once worked with always used the old expression, "You catch more flies with honey than you do with vinegar." Although I could never avoid making the sarcastic come-back, "That assumes you want to catch flies," she was right. No one wants to work with (i.e., *for*) someone who will constantly rub his or her superior status in a subordinate's face. **Z**

D E T A I L S

· · · · · · · · · · · · · · · · · · · ·

ONE OF the most interesting results in the *Principal's Survey of A/E/P and Environmental Consulting Firms* (Mark Zweig & Associates, 1994) is that an increasing number of principals think a single, strong leader is more likely to lead to the firm's success than more democratic forms of management.

In the survey's 1991 edition, about 30% of the principals preferred partnerships, where all decisions are made jointly by partners. The single, strong leader who accepts input, but makes most decisions, received about 29% of the vote. But in 1994, the strong leader took 44% of the vote, to 23% for partnerships.

Mike Beck, president of Fugro East, Inc. (Northborough, MA), a 76-person environmental firm, says his career mirrors that trend. "I think it has more to do with my growth as a manager than a specific philosophy," Beck says. "I think people, as a general rule, are looking for leadership. They're looking for leaders to lead."

Here are some reasons why many principals agree:

Time and money. Management by democratic committee takes much more time, which costs money. A firm could lose its competitive edge, and its people could be less billable. "You get a more balanced viewpoint with committees," says David Wallace, president of Wallace, Floyd Associates, Inc. (Boston, MA), an 80-person architectural firm. "But decisions are made more efficiently with one or two strong leaders."

Hard times. Beck says a down market can prompt principals to change their ways. "It becomes pretty clear what to do when you're having trouble paying the bills," he says.

"Management is looking at itself very critically and is returning to the tradition of strong leadership," says Larry Farrington, VP of finance at Alton Geoscience (Irvine, CA), an 85-person environmental consulting firm.

It helps eliminate finger-pointing. If a decision is wrong, there's only one person to blame. "If a strong leader makes a mistake, he can say 'Hey, I screwed up on this. Here's what we're going to do to fix it,'" says Farrington.

It's respected. Smart people appreciate decisiveness, says Beck. "Sometimes you've just got to say, 'Dammit, this is how it's going to be done,'" he says.

Democratic committees contribute to indecisiveness. This can add stress to even the smallest decision. A principal's view could be clouded by a dozen opinions. The decision might end up being the same, but take days longer to make.

Being a strong leader doesn't mean ignoring other opinions. "A manager can say to his employees, 'I'd like your input.' Within 15 or 20 minutes he gets their input, goes away and makes a decision," says Farrington. "If you're in touch with your staff, they know you're listening. And if you're listening, they know they're not out of the process."

■

Business and architects

FROM time to time, architects and other design professionals all come under fire from the business types for not being sufficiently "business-minded." And, the standard line of defense from those under attack is "I didn't go to school to be a business person. I went to school because I wanted to be an architect." (Or "an engineer.")

The point is well-taken. However, my experience is that if you want to continue being an architect or engineer, you'd better run your business properly. And many *architects*, perhaps because of the artistic nature of their profession, seem to need this kind of reminding more often than some other types of professionals.

My wife and I once went to a friend (and client's) house for a dinner. He is an architect here— a guy with more than 20 years in the business— who only recently started his own firm. By all indications, they've been successful so far. In their first year, they grew to a staff size of five, acquired nice offices, a fully-paid-for CADD terminal in every work station, and lots of work.

After a great "al fresco" dinner of grilled shrimp and chicken, along with several varieties of artfully crafted salads, the last of the wine was poured and the conversation came around to "the business" and to the problem of collecting money.

My friend proclaimed that he did not have any collection problems— that almost all of their clients paid shortly after getting their invoices. All but one, that is— some sort of ego-maniacal businessman with an ocean front house they are renovating.

I had heard something about this particular client a few months back and the first words out of my mouth, almost re-flexively were, "You're not still working for this guy, are you?" fully expecting to hear that they had cut him off.

But to my surprise, he replied, "We are, but it's almost over." He told us in a solemn voice that his client was, in addi-tion to being a "very bad, ruthless" sort of guy, represented by one of the most prominent law firms in Boston. "So what?" I said. He then went on to say that he was afraid to stop work even though this guy hadn't paid him in seven months, be-cause he "didn't want those people on his back."

"Give me a break," I thought to myself. Then I didn't waste the opportunity to fall into what my wife refers to as a "Mark Zweig & Associates" lecture (she has used that expression be-fore when I'm trying to tell her how to do something around the house more efficiently). I told this friend of mine that he was crazy, that if someone doesn't pay his bill, he should be cut off, and that I wouldn't waste *any* time on a bad client. "Turn 'em over in 90 days," I went on, while this guy's poor wife listened.

What's right is right. If a bad client won't pay his bills and it costs more than it's worth to go after him, so be it— you don't have to sue him. But if there is a way to get paid, even if the fee has to be sacrificed to get the money, I think that's a small price to pay for the satisfaction that could come out of it. I'm more fearful that my client will keep working for the crook and get *deeper* in the hole than I am worried he won't get paid for what he's already done so far.

Dealing with people who try to push you around is bad for your psyche. You simply cannot feel good about yourself and have the confidence that it takes to be successful (in the ar-chitectural business or any business, for that matter) when you allow other people to rip you off— the old self-image just can't take it. It is precisely this kind of thinking that is holding all of the design professions back.

No one should have to do work and not get paid for it. If you have agreed to do some scope of work and a client has agreed to pay you, then you *should* get paid. There's not one thing wrong with that. That's the way our system works. There is, however, something *very* wrong when a criminal pushes you around, rips you off, and you line up for more. That's crazy! **Z**

D E T A I L S

· · · · · · · · · · · · · · · · · · · ·

SELF-EMPLOYMENT TEST: Architects were among the first to be laid off when the recession hit a few years ago— and may be the last to go back to work in the still-sluggish economy. The problem: an oversupply of architects and an under-supply of projects.

Many of the laid-off told us they were going into business for themselves as consultants or private practitioners, but we all know that a high percentage of these self-employed architects have no intention of building a business— they're just on an extended job search. "Self employment" has become a euphemism for "unemployment."

Yet, for every ten job-seekers, there is one entrepreneur who's quietly been making the investment necessary to create a viable firm. Despite the lousy business environment, we may be on the verge of a mini-boom of new architecture firms.

However, the problem of how to distinguish between the imitations and the real thing remains. How do you know you're really in business, and not just an unemployed architect? You know when...

■ You hire your first full-time employee, knowing it means you'll make less money yourself over the next few months.

■ You borrow money to buy or lease computers, plotters, and other equipment— the cost of which will take two or three years to pay off or depreciate.

■ You move out of your spare bedroom and sign a lease on some real office space.

■ You see yourself starting to make the same business mistakes your former employer did— and resolve to do it right this time.

■ You turn down a job offer from an established firm because you don't want to work for someone else again.

The bottom line— you know you're really in business when you make a commitment to succeed, stop thinking about fallback positions, and decide there's no going back.

■

NIGHTMARES: Do you have dreams about your work? If so, they're probably nightmares, according to a recent story in The Wall Street Journal.

The story singled out the dreams of two architects— Donald Rattner of Ferguson Murray & Shamamian, Architects (New York, NY) and Kenneth Newberry of Eubank/Bohnn (Houston).

In Rattner's dreams, baseboards in a new house come to life and bang against a kitchen cabinet while blueprint measurements dance around. In Newberry's dreams, floor plans are altered and numbers don't add up. Newberry also dreams he is flying through the air, where he encounters his clients.

■

Calming a complainer

HAVE YOU ever had an employee— one of your best producers— who every so often seems to flip out? It may be once a week, once a month, or once every few months. But one thing's for sure— sooner or later, this person will get totally negative. He'll come into your office and sit down, or he'll catch you in the hall. You'll ask how he is doing and you'll get more than you really wanted in the way of a response. He'll dump a whole truckload of woes on you, and be down on the company, the staff, the clients, or the business as a whole.

If you *have* had one of these people, you've probably said to yourself (and others), "If (John, Steve or Sally) wasn't such a great (architect, engineer, business developer, project manager, etc.), I'd have run him (or her) off years ago." But John, Steve or Sally *is* a great employee— 98% of the time.

Without question, some of the most talented people I've met in this business fit this profile. And many of them *do* eventually leave the company they are complaining about and end up as highly motivated (and vocal) competitors of the firm they left.

What can you do about these people? You don't want them to quit, but you also don't want them to demoralize everyone else in the firm. You don't want to fire them, but you *do* want them to stop bitching and get back to work. I'm not sure there are any easy solutions, but here are my suggestions:

1. **Let the complainer know the negative ramifications of his periodic tirades.** Just like dealing with any problem behavior from an employee, often the best strategy for the manager is confrontation. When it comes to pointing out unacceptable behavior, the earlier in the employer-employee relationship, the better. Letting the complainer have his fits may only reinforce the perception that it is acceptable behavior.

2. **Let him complain— to you and you only.** Maybe letting the complainer blow off steam (to you) is the best strategy for defusing him. You may be able to serve as a cathartic. If you're a good listener, that could be all it takes to make the complainer feel better and get him back to work in a decent frame of mind. But make sure you tell the complainer you are the *only* one who should be hearing this stuff. That it's O.K. for you because you *understand*, but you don't want everyone else in the company exposed to these negative thoughts.

3. **Investigate the complainer's complaint— it may be valid.** I'm sure there were people I worked for who at times thought I was a complainer. But I'll bet my past supervisors, in retrospect, would agree that many of my complaints were valid. Sometimes those who bitch are treated as the problem, when in reality, it is what they are griping about that needs addressing. It's management's job to distinguish what's valid from what's not.

4. **Put the complainer in charge of solving the problem he is griping about.** It's not always a viable option, but there's nothing like this tactic to make a complainer shut up. For example, I have seen this strategy used successfully in a firm where a principal was obsessed with what he thought was poor performance in their marketing group. They made him marketing director and his obsession quickly ended.

Cash is king

THE FIRST rule of business is to *survive*. And when it comes to survival, one of the most relevant statistics to track is *average collection period.*

It doesn't matter how much you sell, how much you bill, or what kind of profit you think you're going to make, if you don't collect the cash, sooner or later you have to borrow to pay your bills. And if you're like most of us, and the amount you can borrow is fixed, then sooner or later, if you don't collect what's owed to you, you're going to run out of credit.

The two kinds of firms most susceptible to variations in cash flow are *small* firms and *growing* firms. Obviously, principals of small *and* growing firms need to be the most vigilant of all. At *least* once per week, managers need to know the company's current and month-to-date cash position plus projections for the next month or so.

We know one small, growing firm that knows its cash position on a *daily* basis, thanks to a simple, one-page report that shows the following:

1. **Cash in:** Cash in since the last report and month-to-date, itemized into fees, reimbursables, and any other category of revenue your firm recognizes.

2. **Cash out:** How much has the company paid out since the last report and month-to-date? Are you spending more than you're collecting?

3. **Current balances:** Show balances for all bank or investment accounts. Also show the company's current line of credit balance (hopefully, zero!).

4. **Projections:** Estimated weekly cash requirements and receipts for the next four weeks. Requirements should be based on accrued expenses already scheduled for payment, plus any expenses that can be anticipated. Receipts should be based on actual payment patterns for each client. Don't try to make things look better than they really are.

5. **Total:** The four week projected requirements and receipts are totaled up. Together with the bank balances, they show principals whether the firm will be able to meet its obligations over the next four weeks.

The financial manager attaches to this report a list of scheduled payments and accounts receivable (sorted by date). Overdue invoices are highlighted.

With a system like this, there are far fewer ugly surprises. When they spot a problem, managers can adjust by delaying a payment or try to speed up collection. And it doesn't need to be computerized. A simple form, filled in by hand, works just fine. **Z**

Consultant or "insultant"?

CHOOSING a good management consultant should be a simple task for any astute design or environmental consulting firm. You send out RFPs asking for proposals, short-list based on those responses, conduct interviews, and negotiate the fee. Just like you get hired by your clients— right?

Wrong. While that approach may work fine for selecting a firm to design a bridge or a new retail store, it's probably not the best way to get a good management consultant. Of course, it all depends on what kind of a management consultant you are looking for. If the task is very clearly defined and the result probably won't be real controversial— such as finding an appraiser for your ESOP, or someone to determine how big the total U.S. market is for asbestos abatement consulting services— that kind of a selection process may be O.K.

If, on the other hand, you are looking for a firm or individual that will help you make a major change in how your firm operates or does business in the future, you may find that the best consultants won't subject themselves to that process.

Dr. Ichak Adizes, in his book *Corporate Lifecycles*, delves into the subject of organizational change and how to effect it. He says internal change agents are doomed from the start (unless they are the majority owners), because in order to be effective, one has to risk alienating one's employer, something no *employee* can afford. That means change agents will probably have to come from outside the company. Adizes dubs these effective change agents "insultants." Insultants, he claims, are the only ones who can be effective because they don't *need* the client.

Common situations in A/E/P and environmental consulting firms that may require an insultant include:

Two or more principals disagree on the firm's direction. This is common, since intelligent people are bound to have different ideas about the firm. A good insultant can flesh out these differences and help sell the right course for the firm to follow.

Too much staff. This is almost always the culprit when a firm needs a significant financial turnaround. The insultant may be best equipped to dispassionately decide who stays and who goes, because he or she has no emotional ties to those who could be affected.

The wrong staff people are in key positions. This, too, is quite common in a professional service firm owned and managed by the same group of people. All too often, those who have been with the firm the longest or those with the most stock end up in positions they aren't qualified for. They may be failing miserably, but no one has the guts to deal with them. Until, that is, the insultant comes into the picture.

Principal salaries are too high. Who is better equipped than an insultant to show principals that the firm cannot afford to pay them what they are taking out? It's certainly not the one-man, self-employed consultant who needs his clients' business so he can make his car payment.

There are others, but the bottom line is the same. Many firms need an insultant. Here are my tips on finding one:

1. **Assume that anyone who goes along with the traditional selection process for consultants as described above is not an insultant.** A good consultant (insultant) stays busy all the time. He won't allow himself to get dragged into a long interview process because he doesn't need it to stay busy. He won't fly to see a client without getting paid. He won't give references before making a

proposal. Anyone who does is telling you they need the work. And if they need the work, they must not be that good.

2. **Look for a successful firm, and someone in that firm who is successful.** If the person isn't successful, they'll need you more than you need them, which is very dangerous. You probably won't get the most out of the experience they acquired working for other firms. They'll instead tell you whatever you want to hear. But be sure the consultant really *is* successful. There are a number of charlatans serving this industry who don't know much about running their own firms. If that's true, how can you expect them to do any better with your firm than they can with their own?

3. **Get someone who may be a little arrogant, a little condescending, etc.** The insultant may, in fact, *put on* that demeanor as a part of his or her act. It may stir the pot and get things out in the open. On the other hand, that demeanor may be nothing more than puffed up *bravado*, and the supposed insultant is just a jerk. Check references and follow your gut.

4. **Ask around.** Who are your competitors using? They have learned something you can benefit from. One of the great things about the A/E/P and environmental consulting business is that most competitors are nice people who will gladly share with you if you simply ask them. **Z**

D E T A I L S

. . . .

MOST principals agree that business planning is essential to running a firm effectively. On the other hand, *not* everyone agrees on whether strategic planning is a "do-it-yourself" project or one requiring expert assistance.

Of course, it's not just the fact of having a consultant that contributes to a better plan. It's knowing *when* to ask for outside help, *how* to choose the right consultant, and *what* to expect.

When the existing process is not working. Several years ago, Fay Spofford & Thorndike (FST), a 200-employee civil engineering firm (Lexington, MA), was experiencing falling revenues, had faced several layoffs, and had not met the lofty goals set in a strategic planning session.

"We realized the way we had been doing business for many years just wasn't going to be the right way to approach the 90s," says Bob Loney, FST president.

Loney says a consultant helped management come up with specific actions to achieve their goals. "Our goals before were kind of like mom and apple pie: 'We want to make more money, we want to be more efficient.' There was no game plan."

When a firm is in transition. When Barbara Cianci-Horton became a partner with Horton-Lees Lighting Design (New York, NY), she saw a need for change. Although the firm had won plenty of awards and done work on four continents, it didn't have an effective marketing strategy, partners were giving staff mixed signals, and some important details— like liability insurance— were being ignored.

Like their own clients, firms have a right to expect concrete results when they hire a consultant. Cianci-Horton credits their business plan with helping the firm weather the recession.

To change management structure. That's what Bucher, Willis & Ratliff, a 200-person E/A firm (Salina, KS), did. The firm also asked for and got concrete results. "If we had gone through all that and spent all the money and all we got was the process, we'd be terribly disappointed," says then firm president, Ray Voskamp.

Other suggestions:

■   The business plan should include a mission, clear strategy statements, concrete goals, and implementation items.

■   If you're going to spend money on a consultant, pick one that will be brutally honest, not the president's golfing buddy.

■   Prepare for your planning session. The consultant must make you face up to hard choices, but it's you who must ultimately take action.

■   Assign specific tasks to staff. The biggest failure of business planning is lack of implementation.

■   Don't accept "motherhood and apple pie." A good plan provides focus.

■

Conventional wisdom isn't always right

CONVENTIONAL WISDOM isn't always so "wise." Let's take a look at some of the wisdom frequently heard in the halls and conference rooms of A/E and environmental consulting firms:

1. **The company will be profitable if every job it takes on is profitable.** This has to be one of the most common misconceptions. The fact is this— you can make a profit on *every* single job you perform and still *lose* money. How can that be? It happens when the firm is not doing it *enough* (in other words, the firm does not have enough work). The firm may do four jobs, all of which make a "profit" based on the project budget, but it really needs eight of these jobs to make a profit *as a company.* What the firm *thinks* is profitable now won't make money in the long term because the real overhead isn't fully factored in.

2. **You can't make money if you take jobs below your break even multiplier.** This, too, is B.S. The error here is assuming that your firm is operating at peak production capacity, which is rarely the case in most firms. The truth is, if you can add *any* revenue without increasing your costs, you'll make money. Consider a firm with 50

employees and a 170% overhead rate. Management figures that it should price services at around 3.02 times raw labor. An opportunity comes in with a 2.0 multiplier and is immediately passed on. But if that 2.0 job can be done by salaried people who do not get paid overtime and the company does not need to add any more staff, it might be foolish to pass on it. Look at how manufacturing firms make pricing decisions— the break even point varies based on plant utilization and capacity.

3. **Every job should go through a formal, go/no-go decision-making process.** This, too, is preposterous, unless a firm does only a few jobs in the course of a year. Most firms are doing lots of jobs with fees in the range of $10,000 to $25,000. We have one client with 200 employees that did over 4,000 projects last year— if they had to make a go/no-go decision on every job, they'd have spent all their time in meetings doing just that.

4. **Proposal and marketing expenses should be tracked by job.** I have vacillated on this issue over the years, but have decided that tracking these costs is usually a waste of time. The real question is: Do you want to go after the job or not, and if so, what do you think you will have to spend to get it? Is the risk worth the potential reward? If so, go for it. Don't waste time trying to collect nickels you can roll into the job cost— charge what the market will bear, no more and no less.

5. **You have to have better-than-average benefits if you want better-than-average employees.** This may make sense for some businesses, but not A/E or environmental consulting firms. When's the last time you heard of a star performer who quit his or her job because the employer didn't provide dental insurance? It's just not happening. I'm more interested in the employee who wants a chance to work hard, take on a lot, and get paid well if the company performs— *not* the one looking for eyewear coverage. Match your benefits to what other firms are doing, but don't try to outdo them.

6. **Today's employees demand flex time.** No doubt, many employees like it, but flex time policies have no place in a design firm. The problem is this: because flex time schedules usually revolve around fitting in your "eight hours" each day, it sets an expectation of a 40-hour work week. And a 40-hour work week for *salaried* people isn't good enough, especially when the most competitive firms in this business have their people working 50 to 55 hours per week. Let those employees who want flex time go to work for another firm and get laid off two years from now when the firm experiences "economic difficulties." I'd rather be employed over the long haul than be home by 4:00 each day for the next year or two so I don't miss *Oprah.*

7. **Satellite offices won't make money for the first couple of years.** I cringe every time I hear this. You can make money right away in a satellite office *if* you match the labor and the overhead to the work you can generate. You will not make money if you rent a lot of space in anticipation of expansion and hire a secretary and three technical people *before* you have the work. Principals who set such low expectations for the performance of satellite offices are the reason too many branch offices don't make any money.

8. **Keeping score causes internal competition, which is bad.** Internal competition can be good if it exposes those people or groups not carrying their weight, inspires people to do more or better work than they would otherwise, or increases the firm's overall success. When I hear people complaining about internal competition, it's usually the ones who head up groups that have 55% utilization rates and 2.35 earned multipliers. The people they are complaining about as too competitive are the ones with 83% utilization rates and 2.95 multipliers. Is the answer to stop measuring so the weak link feels better? I think not. **Z**

D E T A I L S

· · · · · · · · · · · · · · · · · · · ·

INTERNAL competition, just like external competition, is a fact of life. You compete to carve out a secure place for yourself, you compete to be promoted, you compete for bonuses, and so on. There is always going to be internal competition. You can't (and shouldn't want to) stamp it out completely. But what can you do to control it?

"We do not promote internal competition," says Hollis Cheek, president of Attala Lining Systems, Inc. (Kosciusko, MO), a 75-person environmental firm. "We all should be playing on the same team with the same objectives. And that goal and mission should be to do the best job possible for the client, at the most profit."

James L. Sanchez, treasurer/secretary at Pheiler & Associates, Engineers (Diamond Bar, CA), a 15-person consulting engineering firm, agrees. "Competition is good, but I don't like a lot of internal competition," he says. "It's more important to have an atmosphere that feels more like a team, instead of a few individual stars. That's what internal competition can create."

A lack of fair internal competition will keep away or drive away the most motivated professionals, who seek challenges and want recognition above their peers.

Look at who's complaining about internal competition. Are they the people whose performance doesn't measure up? Nobody likes dealing with internal strife. When low performers complain, it may be easier for principals to blame the trouble on "unhealthy internal competition" than to confront the root cause— poor performance. On the other hand, if everyone is dragged down by in-fighting, you probably have created a self-centered, overly competitive climate.

Internal competition is counterproductive when it means pitting people or groups directly against each other on the same task. For one thing, it's redundant— a civil engineering firm doesn't need two highway engineering groups competing for the same job. In addition, people may respond better to competing for goals rather than against each other.

Accountability and rewards are a two-edged sword, and can create healthy or unhealthy competition. Profit-center accounting is perhaps the most controversial promoter of internal competition. We've seen failing firms turn 180 degrees after instituting a performance-based bonus system. We've also seen department and branch managers who sabotage the efforts of other managers to make their own unit look better.

The answer is a bonus system that rewards for unit performance and overall firm performance. The proportion of these two will depend on the current goals of the firm.

The team analogy is used a lot in business. There's always a backup who wants to be a starter— and coaches often play off that emotion to drive both to be better. Yet, both players have the same ultimate goal— for the team to win.

■

Dealing with maturity

ENVIRONMENTAL consulting firms are starting to come to grips with what A/E and consulting engineering firms have faced for years— a mature marketplace. No longer is the demand for environmental services growing at a 10-20% annual rate. The whole industry is in a crisis.

Meanwhile, just because architects and engineers have been dealing with a mature market (or a declining one, in some cases) for 10 or more years, it doesn't mean they've *all* found the answers yet. Some firms have— firms like Mid-State Associates, Inc. (Baraboo, WI), which has grown to over 200 employees with offices in towns of less than 12,000 people, or Carter & Burgess, Inc. (Fort Worth, TX), which more than tripled in size over a four-year period, or ADD, Inc. (Cambridge, MA), a 40-person architectural firm that declined in size but stayed profitable the entire time. Not everyone is doing so well, however.

The point is, now we're all in the same boat. But some firms have figured out how to *succeed* in spite of the market. Let's take a look at some of the tactics successful A/E, consulting engineering, and environmental consulting firms are using today to make money in a mature marketplace (much to the chagrin of their competitors):

1. **They're actively recruiting the best possible staff.** This includes experienced employees working for competitors,

as well as new hires coming from client organizations or regulatory agencies who can bring in work.

2. **They're streamlining their organization and reporting structures.** I sound like a broken record on this one, but the matrix is dead. Even the giant Digital Equipment Corporation has thrown out the matrix in an effort to restore profitability. The companies that are able to deal with a mature marketplace are focusing on restoring accountability through single-person reporting. They're also trying to renew client focus by setting themselves up to address the needs of particular client sectors (sector being defined as a group of buyers with common wants and needs). And they're saying goodbye to the "old" discipline-based structures or those set up strictly along geographical lines (the Southwest, Pacific states, etc.).

3. **They're positioning themselves as specialists in one or more market sectors.** The more mature the market, the more critical it is to be perceived as having specialized knowledge. Only in new or fast-growing service markets does the *technology* drive the consultant selection process— as environmental firms are just now figuring out.

4. **They're keeping their eye on the business.** In a mature market, you can't always cure your woes by growing the organization. You have to figure out how to run it profitably based on the work that you *can* get. Mature markets require a new focus on the operations end of the business, not just the marketing end. Management must pay much closer attention to the numbers— including profits and cash flow.

5. **They're moving closer to their clients.** In a mature market, being close to the client may be the determining factor in whether or not you get the job. There seems to be more willingness again to have small satellite offices to accomplish this. What's different in a mature market versus a growing one is that these small satellite offices are

keeping overhead way down in order to make a profit on what may not be a lot of work.

6. **They're advancing technologically, not retreating.** The "old" way of dealing with a declining market was to re-trench and cut back on expenses, particularly capital investments. The "new" way is to charge ahead and improve technological capabilities so the firm can become more efficient and competitive. That's the difference between long-range success and short-range success.

7. **They're improving their marketing support capabilities.** Just like investments in technology, investments in marketing support capabilities are important, too, and bear fruit in the long haul. This means the secretary who rose to marketing manager during the good times may no longer be adequate to keep the firm on top of its game in a mature market. It means that having a good marketing database and good writing, graphic design, and PR capabilities are more critical than ever.

My best advice to any firm experiencing the trauma of a mature market is to look at the companies that are doing well in spite of it, and consider doing what they're doing. Or, in other words, model success. **Z**

D E T A I L S

- - - - - - - - - - - - - - - - - - - -

ENVIRONMENTAL MARKET NOT IMPROVING: The outlook for the U.S. environmental consulting and engineering market continues to deteriorate, according to an annual study by market researchers Farkas Berkowitz & Co. (Washington, DC) and reported in *Hazardous Waste Business* in April of 1994.

"Nearly every sector showed clear signs of maturity that had been masked by the 1990-1991 recession and the subsequent slow economy. The U.S. market continues to experience slow growth, modest profitability and the tougher competition brought on by over-capacity," says the report.

Among the findings:

■ Hazardous waste consulting revenues plateaued in 1993 and will now decline. Environmental consulting, a $9 billion market, did not grow in 1993. Environmental remediation ($7 billion) was a wash, with higher demand at lower prices.

■ Ten firms account for 25% of all environmental consulting and engineering billings: Camp Dresser & McKee (Cambridge, MA), CH2M HILL, Inc. (Denver, CO), Dames & Moore (Los Angeles, CA), ERM Group (Exton, PA), ICF Kaiser (Fairfax, VA), International Technology Corp. (Torrance, CA), Montgomery Watson (Pasadena, CA), Roy F. Weston, Inc. (West Chester, PA), Rust International (Birmingham, AL), and Woodward-Clyde Group, Inc. (Denver, CO).

■ Prices for lab services have declined 5% to 10% annually since 1990. Many providers got out of the business in 1993.

■ The industrial Superfund market is on hold for several years "as PRP committees wait for a statutory framework with a better deal."

■ In the much-ballyhooed Department of Defense remediation market, it appears that contracts issued will exceed actual demand, as most bases have six or more contracts to choose from.

■ In the international market, U.S. firms will face tough competition from each other, other industrialized nations, and from new companies in the developing countries.

■

HOW DO you know when the market for what you do has matured?

■ Your effective raw labor multiplier drops from 3.6, to 3.2, to 2.8, to 2.3.

■ You have to submit 27 proposals to get one job.

■ You have not seen "limitation of liability" in a contract for years.

■ Your employment ads in the Sunday paper produce bushel baskets of qualified candidates.

■ The first thing your client wants to know is what your price is.

■ Making cold calls is essential to your firm's survival.

■ You haven't had a raise or bonus in three years.

■

Debriefing— the right way

A COMMONLY heard marketing tip is to debrief a potential client when your firm is not selected for a job. Marketers say what you learn can improve proposals and increase hit rates.

"There's a real need to follow up to find out why you won or lost," says Fred Kisner, regional marketing director at Tetra Tech, Inc. (Pasadena, CA), a 700-person environmental consulting firm. "Maybe you proposed a Cadillac and they wanted a Yugo. Or vice versa."

More than 90% of firms debrief clients when they don't get a job, according to the 1994 *Marketing Survey of A/E/P and Environmental Consulting Firms* (Mark Zweig & Associates). Half of them do it always or often. But still only about one in four proposals submitted by A/E/P and environmental consulting firms are successful, the survey says. If debriefing is so effective, why are hit rates so low?

Maybe it's because so few firms put sufficient emphasis on the process and so few ask the right questions. They're not doing it right!

Here are suggestions for a successful debriefing process:

Do it every time, even when you *win*. "Sometimes" or "often" isn't enough. If you really want to improve your proposals, get a full-fledged assessment *every time*. "Somebody high up in the organization has to demand that information as a normal part of the overall proposal process," says Kisner. "Until the debrief is done, you're not done with that proposal, whether you win or lose."

Make it clear you're looking for information, not trying to change the client's mind. Michael Wright, vice president of Medical Cities, Inc. (Dallas, TX), a 500-person contractor of health care facilities, says design and consulting firms that bid on his projects rarely call after losing out on a job. When they do, he says, they often put him on the defensive.

"If someone is really interested in finding out why they didn't get the job, not in an antagonistic manner, we're happy to talk to them," says Wright. "But the decision is made and we're not going to change it."

Don't pass the job down the ranks. Wright says he appreciates it much more when a *principal* takes the time to call seeking feedback. "Having a good, healthy conversation helps cement a relationship," he says. "Maybe they weren't right this time, but that doesn't mean they won't be next time around."

Encourage complete honesty. "Sometimes you get a legitimate response and sometimes you get a fairy tale," says William Hemsley, president at Nassaux-Hemsley, Inc. (Chambersburg, PA), a 40-person consulting engineering firm. "When they tell you the truth, the procedure can be beneficial."

Often, you'll discover that the selection process was politically motivated or the winning firm had some other kind of insurmountable advantage. "A lot of times we just get the fluff answers," says Joseph McGovern, director of business development at B.A. Leisch & Associates (Minneapolis, MN), a 60-person environmental consulting firm. "And a lot of times when politics are behind it, you just get B.S. answers."

Put in an effort that corresponds to the significance of the client. In most cases, a phone call from a principal is sufficient. But some clients may warrant more. Rob Barrick, president and CEO at Smith Seckman Reid, Inc. (Nashville, TN), a 170-person consulting engineering firm, says his firm will sometimes visit a client to conduct a debriefing. "The CEO usually calls the guy who gets the job, and passes it off to someone to call everyone else," says Barrick. "If you call that guy who gives you the bad news and say, 'Not only are we *not* mad, we'd like to keep working with you,' he's going to be much more willing to help you."

If you lose, find out who won and why. The "who" is usually well known. Finding out the "why" is harder. Kisner says he once called a client after not getting a job and was told the other firm was more qualified for that particular project. But when he called the winning firm about another matter, he discovered the firm was *less* qualified than his, but had worked with the client before. "They knew them and liked them," says Kisner. "It had nothing to do with that specific project. But no client is going to tell you that."

Develop a list of questions and stick to it. Sometimes debriefing calls start off in the right direction, then wander. Write up a list of questions and make sure you ask most of them.

Don't ignore feedback. Kisner suggests keeping a database of debriefing responses for easy access. When you're considering a proposal to a client you've solicited before, you can check back and find out what they like or dislike. And if five different clients make the same comment about your proposals, change them. **Z**

D E T A I L S

HOW CAN you increase your odds of getting selected for state departments of transportation work? Here's what several DOT officials told us.

Read the project description information very carefully, and tailor your proposal to what's written. A lot of DOT announcements look the same, but contain subtle differences that could change the way you approach your statement of interest or proposal. Max Landes, chief of consulting services for the Illinois DOT (Springfield, IL), says he is frustrated by firms that don't read the proposal thoroughly. "I'm sure they get tired of reading that stuff, but sometimes we make changes and people don't seem to be reading them," says Landes.

Forrest Smith, contracting officer for the Colorado DOT (Denver, CO), says some firms mistakenly try to duplicate proposals that worked in the past. "If you say 'The reason I got the project last time was *xyz*,' and you really focus on *xyz* the next time, you could lose the project altogether," he says.

Pick your spots. Landes says he sees too many firms "checkerboarding"— submitting on every kind of job, even if the firm really isn't qualified to do it. "I'll call a firm to talk about a submission, and the project manager whose name is on it won't even know his name is on there," he says. "That's happened a hundred times."

Get technical input on the proposal. Landes says he can tell when a proposal was written solely by someone in marketing, with little input from a technical person. "I don't think marketing people have enough knowledge of that kind of information," he says.

Make sure the right people are listed on the project team. Smith says poor team selection is a common error. "You have to analyze the project and determine who's right for that project," he says.

Give the right amount of information. Firms often give more or less information than the situation calls for. For this reason, many states limit how much information a firm can submit in the early stages of the proposal process— right down to the size of the type in some cases.

Mark Wilson, contractual services engineer for the Florida DOT (Tallahassee, FL), says that state requires firms to submit a maximum *two-page* letter of response on projects it advertises. That forces firms to stick to the point, he says.

Keep visible. No matter how much work you've done with the DOT in the past, you can't let your firm slide out of the minds of the important people. Check in regularly with DOT managers to make sure projects in progress are going as smoothly as they can. Finally, principals and project managers should remain active in professional organizations and state-sponsored programs like seminars and conferences.

Debunking marketing myths

AVE YOU SEEN the bumper sticker that says "Question Authority?" Well now's the time to question conventional wisdom with respect to marketing A/E and environmental consulting services.

Many of the "experts" both inside and outside of A/E, consulting engineering, and environmental firms (those who have read all of the latest management books) are perpetuating falsehoods about marketing for our industry. Following are ten of these frequently heard marketing myths that need clearing up:

1. **Specialized firms are hit hardest when the market they serve declines.** On the surface, this seems logical. If an A/E or environmental firm is dependent on one market (a specific group of clients, not a technology or technical discipline area), why wouldn't they suffer right along with their market? One reason is that they will *anticipate* what is happening to their market before those who just dabble in it. Whether that means early warning to find a new specialty, or the know-how to develop new services, pricing structures, and distribution channels for this same market, they'll react faster and better.

2. **Marketing people are supposed to sell.** Part of the confusion over this subject lies in a misunderstanding about the real meaning of marketing. There may be business development or sales people who sell (both business development and sales are subsets of the broader subject of marketing), but there are more marketing people who don't. But just because they aren't selling, don't think they aren't important. Marketing in our business requires teamwork. Although clients, by and large, want to deal with the technical people who can solve their problem, marketing people can get the phone ringing and then help the sellers close.

3. **It takes seven (or five, or six, or eight) contacts to make a sale.** This is just plain false. I have personally made a sale on the first or second contact on a number of occasions. These kinds of statistics are cooked up by people who want an excuse for their poor performance in a selling role.

4. **You have to make cold calls to be successful.** The most successful people in this business never make a cold call. They don't have to. Their phone rings and they respond. Smart A/E and environmental consulting firms are *investing* in the things that make their phones ring, like a good database, direct mail, market research, new services, and industry-specific P.R., *not* putting all of their money and time into trying to get expensive professional and technical people to make largely ineffective cold calls.

5. **You have to have done "X" number of similar projects to get a job.** If this were true, how would any firm ever get off the ground? *Somebody* has to be first. If you can convey to the client that you understand his or her needs better than anyone else, and you won't be learning at the client's expense, costing more money, or causing any headaches, they'll hire you without bushel baskets of similar projects in your history.

6. **Being a "TQM" firm gives you a selling advantage.** The U.S. A/E and consulting engineering industry has always lagged behind big business. And it's not because we're slow or stupid, but because we're fractionated. We don't have one primary source for information on these subjects, so things take longer to filter down to us. Many *other* businesses (e.g., manufacturers, process industries, high tech firms— even some government entities) have already been through TQM. It came after the last new management religion their leaders forced on them, and has already been replaced by corporate re-engineering and the total solution (complete integration of all systems). No one could argue with the main tenets of TQM. But because it has already been tried and failed in so many of our *clients'* organizations, those clients may actually be *laughing* at your wide-eyed zeal for TQM.

7. **Proposal covers should be standardized.** Thousands of things *need* standardization in our firms, but this is the one that we actually do? Don't give every client the same old boring proposal cover. Be different, be bold. Make your proposals stand out, not blend in with the 200 or so others that the client may get.

8. **Newsletters should only go out quarterly.** Trying to do them more frequently makes it too difficult for your technical people to keep up with the demand for articles. Plus it's too expensive. Baloney! Many of the newsletters we see share the same problems. They're aimed at no one in particular. They're expensive to print because they are too long and use color photography. And they do little more than brag about past projects with long, overly technical treatises, or list who was promoted to senior associate. Firms should cut the length, increase the frequency, and get rid of the floss and gloss. Instead of using technical people to write articles on projects, get a *writer* to interview clients, potential clients, and regulatory officials who have something to offer *one* specific, targeted audience.

9. **Every firm could benefit from becoming more *proactive* in its marketing.** Wrong. If you can't *close* the opportunities that are already coming your way, why create more (that you won't close anyway)? Maybe the sales problem comes from not reacting properly, and the firm, because it has limited resources, should be more *reactive*.

10. **A good brochure is important to your marketing.** The last thing most firms should do is spend time and money on a brochure. The typical firm (especially if it has more than one owner) takes from two to five years to do a brochure! And when it's done, it gets mailed to the Christmas card list (because the firm won't spend money on a client database), which by and large is made up of the firm's suppliers and competitors. Clients who get the brochure throw it in a file never to be looked at again, or worse, in the trash.

Let's all start to question the authority of those preaching the same old tired marketing gospel for our industry, and act accordingly. **Z**

Defining "partner"

WITH ALL the management consulting we do for A/E/P and environmental consulting firms, we commonly find misconceptions about what it means to be a partner. When I say *partner* (in this industry), that doesn't necessarily mean you work in a *partnership*— the term is synonymous with "principal" in the typical, closely held professional service firm, even if the company is legally organized as a *corporation*.

A good example of a misconception surrounding the role would be the discovery I once made of a partner who didn't think he had to fill out a time sheet. As a result, none of his time was ever billed to a job. Or the partner who thought she was above having a vacation accrual account. She thought she was entitled to take off whenever she wanted. Or how about the partner in a 15-owner firm who was upset because the company grew so large he could no longer set the salary for a drafter in an office 600 miles away? That's crazy, too. To me, being a partner means that you:

Build on the strengths of the individuals who make up the partnership. Individual partners have to assume roles that capitalize on their best qualities. For example, if so-and-so is good at selling, she should be selling. If so-and-so is good with financial matters, he should assume the CFO role.

Compensate for the weaknesses of those who make up the partnership. No two people can make the same contribution to the company. If "Johnson" is terrible at dealing with underlings, get him out of that role. If "Smith" cannot write a decent letter, make sure someone else reviews all of her correspondence.

Help each other. The desire to help each other in times of need is essential to a functional partnership. That means you don't try to make your partner look bad by attacking him or her at the first sign of weakness. All partners in a firm are in the same boat, and people *do* have their ups and downs. You need to be there for the other guy when he needs you.

Do your share. A good partner does everything within his power to make sure he is carrying his own weight— all the time. This means he stays billable if that's his job, sells if that's his job, or runs a profitable office or department if that's his job. He does whatever is necessary to justify his existence in the company. He doesn't want to have to ask his fellow partners to bail him out of jams that he created, or to make up for his lack of performance.

Being a partner does *not* mean:

All rewards are shared equally. Again, not everyone can contribute equally to the partnership. Some strengths are more highly sought after than others. Some partners brought more start-up capital to the firm. Some partners are simply more critical to the company's success. These people need to get paid more than other partners, even though the others *are* partners, and *are* important to the firm.

All decisions are made as a group and unanimously. I don't know where this idea originated— probably from a second generation firm where none of the founder's successors would step up as the leader. Many partners in multi-owner firms have the warped idea that being a partner means you have to make all decisions as a group, and that everyone *always* has to agree. This culture will virtually destroy a company, as decision-making will eventually get so time-consuming that the company simply cannot respond to its environment.

You can coast as much as you want. I cannot tell you how many times I have run into this attitude. It's even been verbalized to me as "I busted my butt for years to get where I am, now I'm entitled to enjoy the fruits of my labor." Balderdash! *Every* partner has to justify his or her existence *every* day, just like any other employee. When too many partners start to think like this, the company goes down the toilet—fast.

You aren't accountable to anyone else. I love the organization charts that look like everyone works for all the partners, and the partners report to no one. I can tell you, it doesn't work. Everyone needs to have somebody to report to, even the CEO. The CEO works for the Board of Directors or all of the owners.

You can meddle in anyone else's affairs. This kind of thinking is very destructive because it breaks down the bond of trust that has to be there between partners. If partners are second-guessing each other and poking their noses into every decision their partners make, one or more things happen—the company stops making decisions, partners become demotivated, or they become unwilling to accept responsibility for anything.

More firms in this business should spend quality time defining and understanding what it means (or doesn't mean) to be a partner, if they want to survive and prosper over the long haul. **z**

D E T A I L S

MOST A/E/P and environmental consulting firms have no system in place to evaluate principals. Do they need one?

Norm Johnson, vice president and manager of the Longwood, Florida office of 160-person consulting engineering firm Johnson Mirmiran & Thompson, P.A. (Sparks, MD), believes they do. A sub-par principal at his former firm lingered for several years before finally getting fired. "They had no rating schedule whatsoever for their principals, and it was devastating to the company," says Johnson.

Here's a look at who's reviewing principals:

Peers. At USKH (Anchorage, AK), a 90-person consulting engineering firm, all employees are reviewed annually, including principals. CEO Leo von Scheben says principals are reviewed by a pair of fellow principals. "It's hard to do one-on-one," says von Scheben. "Sometimes it can be intimidating for the guy getting reviewed. But in the long run, you have better communication two-on-one because you have different perspectives."

Subordinates. Michael Fox, president of Michael Fox, Inc. (St. Louis, MO), an 18-person architectural and interior design firm once asked all the firm's employees to review the principals. "I think it may have had more internal P.R. impact than anything else," he says. "In most cases, people given the opportunity to review principals' performances were a little bit shy. As I remember it, they turned their attention more toward firm-wide things."

In general, subordinates may have insights about how principals are doing, but they are not in a position to, and shouldn't be asked to *evaluate* principals' overall performance.

The "numbers." Bob Wuertz, principal at Project Associates, Inc. (Evansville, IN), says principals are reviewed in his firm based on the work they bring in and their contribution to the firm's profitability. Several factors are taken into consideration, particularly the type of client each principal is working with. "If you do that, history will show us how everyone is doing," says Wuertz.

No one. "I don't review principals," says Wes Lowder, president of The Mehlburger Firm (Little Rock, AK), a 40-person architectural firm. "They're principals of this firm because they've already demonstrated an ability to think for themselves." Lowder says he and his principals have "frank discussions" about how to improve business, but no formal process. And what about the rare principal who is not performing up to the standards at Mehlburger? "That review is 'How long do you need to clear out your desk?'" Lowder says.

Look for more principals to be accountable to *someone* in the future. Despite efforts by some firms to create an environment where everyone is more or less equal, there should be a double standard on performance in design and environmental consulting firms— principals should be held to a *higher* standard.

■

Designing an invoice

Y OU'VE heard it a thousand times. A well-designed invoice is the first step to getting paid. But how do you know if an invoice is "well-designed?" Actually, it's a fairly simple process— a well-designed invoice includes all the important information, and is easy to understand. Period.

A professional invoice has a *date*, a *number*, and is labeled *invoice*. It also explains clearly what work has been done and what the client owes you. It is *signed*, and includes a *name*, and *phone number* of someone the client can call with a question.

A poorly designed invoice is confusing, contains a lot of excess detail, and doesn't clearly state what has been done, and what is owed. It doesn't include a signature or phone number, so it might sit on a desk until *you* call to see why it's not paid.

The invoice below meets our test of an effective invoice. If your invoices aren't getting the results they should, try these suggestions. It may help you get paid faster. **Z**

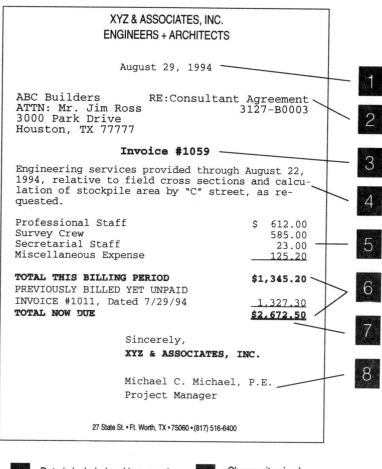

XYZ & ASSOCIATES, INC.
ENGINEERS + ARCHITECTS

August 29, 1994

ABC Builders   RE:Consultant Agreement
ATTN: Mr. Jim Ross   3127-B0003
3000 Park Drive
Houston, TX 77777

Invoice #1059

Engineering services provided through August 22,
1994, relative to field cross sections and calcu-
lation of stockpile area by "C" street, as requested.

Professional Staff	$ 612.00
Survey Crew	585.00
Secretarial Staff	23.00
Miscellaneous Expense	125.20
TOTAL THIS BILLING PERIOD	**$1,345.20**
PREVIOUSLY BILLED YET UNPAID	
INVOICE #1011, Dated 7/29/94	1,327.30
TOTAL NOW DUE	**$2,672.50**

Sincerely,
XYZ & ASSOCIATES, INC.

Michael C. Michael, P.E.
Project Manager

27 State St. • Ft. Worth, TX • 75060 • (817) 516-6400

1 Date is included and in a prominent place for easy reference

2 Project/contract clearly
identified

3 Clearly marked "Invoice," and
includes a reference number

4 Clear explanation of the work
you have done

5 Charges itemized

6 Totals for bills in bold type so it
is easy to see what is owed

7 "Total Now Due" includes previously billed, unpaid invoices

8 Invoice is signed so client can
see you have looked at it personally, and can identify someone to call with questions

Effective satellite offices

I HAVE tremendous respect for any A/E/P or environmental firm that has learned to successfully manage a network of satellite or branch offices. It's not easy.

There's no question that having multiple offices greatly complicates this business, as any CEO knows. How can you keep control over the work quality put out by a branch? How much rope should you give the manager? Too much, and he might hang himself. Not enough, and he can blame you for failure. What do you do to make sure the people in the remote offices feel like they are a part of the overall company? How can a typical branch be competitive when it has the overhead of a big firm, but the locally based capability of a small firm?

These issues, and many more, require constant attention from top management. Here are some things that are important to the successful management of branch offices:

1. **The office manager has to buy into the firm's culture.**
   It helps if the manager has worked at the headquarters, but that's not always possible. Local market knowledge is often essential for a satellite office to sell its own work, which means the manager probably *hasn't* worked at headquarters. But you can bring the manager to the home office frequently. Your principals can go see him. And you can include him in the overall business planning process.

2. **Get a manager who assumes responsibility for generating work for his office.** The last thing you want is a manager who sees his role as caretaker of an office that is a consumer of man-hour budgets on projects sold by others. If that's how it works, why have the office? This mentality prohibits success.

3. **Track sales and profits by office.** Don't let those who claim this process causes unhealthy competition keep you from holding people accountable for performance. Usually, those opposed to this kind of measurement aren't carrying their weight.

4. **Link up electronically and have appropriate policies that reinforce the use of underutilized staff, no matter where they are located.** This is essential to moving work between offices, a requirement for profitability. Not being linked electronically virtually ensures problems in quality and production efficiency from work that is divided up or passed back and forth. And even though each office must create its own work, there may be times that a peak needs shaving or a valley needs filling. One way to do that is move people. Underutilized staff should be used in any role they can fill, even if it's not the highest or best use of their capabilities, and even if they are not ideally qualified for the job, as long as quality doesn't suffer.

5. **Don't ignore little things that demotivate satellite office managers and their employees.** I'm talking about the common practice of not including branch office employees in the internal company newsletter, or putting the headquarters office address in big, bold letters and the satellite office addresses in tiny letters on all "corporate" marketing pieces that are supposed to help branch offices. Another thing that upsets satellites is getting hand-me-down surveying equipment or clapped-out company cars as that stuff is replaced with new equipment in the main office— a big demotivator!

6. **Confront any office manager who uses animosity toward corporate as his primary motivational tactic.** Office managers who rally their troops by focusing on the internal enemy called "corporate" or "headquarters" cannot be tolerated. While this tactic does work, sometimes for quite a while, the divisiveness it creates can eventually tear a company apart. I can't tell you how many times I have seen this culture in a satellite office lead to an eventual coup attempt or separation of the office from the rest of the company.

7. **Allocate corporate overhead to the satellites.** On one hand, I can see why satellite office managers gripe about their corporate overhead allocations. The typical remote office has a hard time competing with similar-sized, locally owned operations that have lower overhead. And the support these satellites get from corporate isn't always fantastic, nor are the benefits of what corporate is doing effectively sold to the satellite office managers. But the costs of operating a multi-office business are real. And in many cases, if the satellite were to independently contract for the services it gets from the home office, the total cost would be higher than it is under the allocation. Firms that don't allocate overhead often have branch offices that think they're more profitable than they are. Then, when they don't get the share of the profits they feel they deserve at bonus time (based on an inflated profit figure), it fuels their animosity toward the home office.

No doubt, the headaches of running a multi-office A/E/P or environmental firm are real. But doing so is essential for most principals to achieve their goals. **Z**

D E T A I L S

. . . .

MORE ON SATELLITES: A reader (who asked to remain anonymous) wrote to suggest an additional point to our article on satellite offices ("Effective satellite offices"— see preceding pages).

"Educate your HQ staff to approach their relationship with the branch office folks as if they were clients who required timely and cordial service. While principals are making visits to the branch offices and officers are interacting at planning and marketing meetings, the HQ support staff (receptionist, secretaries, accounting staff, business development staff) can undermine all progress made by taking every opportunity to let branch office personnel know 'who's boss.'

"This happens when branch personnel call in to ask questions about such items as benefits, a billing status, and their paycheck stub, and are read the riot act by the HQ support staff.

Instead of taking time to find out how they can help the branch office staff member work with the systems in place and educating them on what HQ has to offer them, the HQ support staff takes the opportunity to 'tell' their 'teammate' about all the procedures they did not follow, how they are not going to get what they want until they do, and if they do not like it they can see their boss, because he will back HQ procedures.

"Educate HQ staff that the whole value of centralized support is to save time and money, and coordinate the team's efforts. Therefore, their value as support staff lies in the degree to which they give quality service to the branches, forge positive and reciprocal working relationships, and, in a sense, get repeat business when branch offices call in to get help before something happens instead of being 'discovered' after procedures are not followed."

■

HOW CAN firms load the dice in favor of opening satellite offices that will be successful?

According to the *Satellite Office Survey of A/E/P & Environmental Consulting Firms* (MZ&A, August 1994), placing a principal or owner in charge of a start-up satellite office was the surest path to success— 64% of the most successful satellite offices represented in the survey were started with an owner or principal as the leader. Conversely, 61% of the offices described as "least successful" were started with a non-owner or non-principal in charge.

Three-quarters of the most successful offices were also started with pre-existing work, a so-called "hot start." Of course, a hot start is no guarantee that an office will be successful. More than half the offices described as "least successful" also had a hot start.

Jose Novoa, president of 160-person E/A firm, Halff Associates, Inc. (Dallas, TX) *prefers* a cold start. "It tends to develop a broader base of clients earlier— you're not dependent on just one client...managers learn to hustle earlier in their life," he says.

■

Employee credo

ALTHOUGH I DISLIKE corny slogans and management propaganda, one of our fast-growing clients asked me recently if we had some sort of "employee credo" they could provide to new staff.

This firm's owners were concerned that new people were taking too long to learn their corporate culture. They wanted to speed up the indoctrination process. They needed something that would clearly and succinctly tell their staff— professional, technical and non-technical— how to act (i.e., what the expectation is for behavior in their firm).

Realizing their firm really wasn't much different from any well-run A/E, consulting engineering or environmental consulting firm, we decided to share the end product with readers:

"XYZ Associates Employee Credo"

1. **I understand the entire reason our firm exists is to fulfill needs in client organizations.** We are here because of our clients, not vice versa. I will constantly be on the lookout for ways to make our firm more valuable to clients.

2. **I understand our firm is in the business of providing professional services.** I will constantly analyze my activities to make sure they contribute to the process of sell-

ing, doing, or getting paid for this service. If I am not enhancing this process, I will either stop what I am doing or bring it to management's attention.

3. **I understand I work in a for-profit enterprise and profits are essential to our survival.** I accept responsibility for seeing to it that my employment contributes to profitability.

4. **I understand I am working to build an organization that will outlast any of us as individuals.** I will constantly think about everything I do and whether or not I am contributing to more than just the short-term prosperity of the firm. I will seek to provide some sort of residual benefit that will accrue to the company from each of my actions today.

5. **I understand in an organization that sells time for a living, the product being sold is me.** I recognize that my value to the firm is based on how many productive hours I can generate, how quickly or efficiently I can complete my assignment, or how I can help someone else complete their job.

6. **I will do all I can to ensure output is of the highest quality and is what it is represented to be.** But I recognize that in spite of our best intentions as individuals and as an organization, mistakes will occur. As soon as a mistake is identified, I will immediately acknowledge it and take corrective action.

7. **I understand in any organization there may be times when certain jobs need doing that are unpleasant, tedious, or do not come naturally, yet are necessary.** I will do these jobs if requested to do so or if I see that they need doing, without hesitation or complaint.

8. **I understand a company is like a family.** The needs of the family take precedence over the needs of any one family member, and all family members must contribute to the well-being of the family in an "all for one, one for all" spirit.

9. **I understand that what I say and do affects the morale and productivity of others in the firm.** I will refrain from sarcastic comments that demean the firm, fellow employees, clients, or the output of the firm in any way, and I expect to be treated in like manner.

10. **I will be honest, and not lie, cheat or steal from the firm or its clients.** In return, I expect to be treated truthfully and honestly by management.

11. **I understand that while I have a responsibility to management, management has an equal responsibility to me.** If at any time I unknowingly stray from the principles that built the organization, it is management's duty to bring this to my attention. My commitment to the firm will be returned in equal measure by management's commitment to me. I will be recognized for my past, present and future contributions to the firm.

12. **Last, I understand that my employment at this firm means that I accept all the tenets of this credo and that they will also be recognized and accepted by all other members of the firm.** Management will not tolerate a double standard and will enforce adherence to the credo.

While you may or may not agree with all of the points in this credo, maybe you should spend some time developing your own. Whatever you come up with, don't forget that the best professionals are intelligent people who will not tolerate being manipulated by management. **Z**

D E T A I L S

▪ ▪

I THINK we've all gotten pretty tired of those corny motivational posters you see advertised in the airline magazines. You know the ones I'm talking about— they'll say "Winning," and have a picture of a racing car streaking by at 190, or "Effort," and show an Olympic pole vaulter's determined face as he crosses over the bar.

While I'm sure the creators of these posters are well intentioned, and I *do* like most of their messages, professional engineers, architects, and landscape architects may get turned off by them. Too often, they see these things as just one more attempt from management to manipulate them, so they backfire.

Following are a few things you can put up on the wall that may actually have a positive motivational effect:

1. *Company financial performance.* Most employees really appreciate being kept informed about how well the firm is doing. They want to know things like net revenues, earned multiplier, utilization rates, profitability (or lack of it), sales, backlog, and average collection period. Posting these and other quantifiable indicators of how well the firm is doing throughout the company reduces management's need to tell people what to do.

2. *Sales victories.* There's not much more motivational than getting recognized for selling a job, unless it's *not* being included on a list of people who *have* sold work during a particular period. We shouldn't have such a problem in the A/E/P and environmental consulting business with singling out those who sell work.

3. *Best idea of the month.* This may be perceived as corny by some. But maybe suggestion box programs fail because companies rarely provide feedback to the employees on those suggestions. Single out the best one periodically and post it for all to see. Better yet, post the original suggestion with a description of how it was implemented and what the results were, all on one sheet of paper.

4. *Accolades from a client.* Everybody likes it when a client seems appreciative of the work the company has performed, so why not let everyone know when it happens? Have a regular section on the company bulletin board to post these letters when they come in. Make a big deal out of it and maybe your staff will see that having happy clients really *is* important to you.

5. *The company mission statement, signed by all principals.* A number of A/E/P and environmental firms have done this. They put a poster-size version of the mission up and get all the principals to hand-sign it. That makes it a little more memorable than it would be if it were sitting on the CEO's bookshelf.

■

Evidence of change

ATTENDED a meeting not long ago at Harold Johnson School, where my daughter is a student in the second grade. Parents were invited to come and talk about "what they would do if they were the principal." It was a good opportunity to participate in my daughter's education, so I went.

There's been a lot going on in our town. The Morse Institute Library, a Gothic Revival structure in downtown Natick, is being more than doubled in size and completely renovated. We are getting a new municipal complex for the town government, fire and police departments. We have several new restaurants, and the Natick Mall has just re-opened after Homart bought the old mall, tore it down, and built a new one in its place— and it's the most successful mall opening in their history. High-tech companies Cognex and Boston Scientific have just moved to town, bringing more than 700 new jobs. Clark's Block building, an impressive 60,000 square foot office/retail building downtown, built in the 1870s, is even getting new, architecturally correct windows.

Our schools, too, are getting a lot of new attention. Johnson School has a new principal, a former entrepreneur who owned a successful electrical contracting firm, Kevin Crowley. He's a lot different from our last principal, who was a nice fellow, but not a "shake-em-up" leader. This guy sees no obstacle he cannot overcome.

The problem is that Johnson School's existence is being threatened. Because the building is the oldest of Natick's five elementary schools, the school committee could decide to close it and relocate the kids to another school, or build a new school somewhere else. Because the school's survival is at stake, we thought it would be good to show the community some physical evidence of the change going on inside the school.

The relevance of all this to our readers is that the situation at Johnson is not unlike the situation in many A/E/P or environmental firms that are reinventing themselves right now. Management may know that it's not "business as usual," but employees and clients, as well as the community at large, need to have that message driven home.

Here are some of the ideas we talked about at the Johnson School meeting for communicating the school's new vitality:

1. **Paint the building.** If you want to show you are different on the inside, you have to look different on the outside. A number of parents (and the principal) thought painting the old, brown brick of the school's quaint architectural exterior white, putting on some bright accent colors, and maybe a mural on the outside, would help rejuvenate the school's image. Ditto for replacing the chain-link fence with a white picket fence. Firms going through a leadership change should take note.

2. **Get a new sign.** Some of us who have lived here for years have taken for granted that everyone knows where Johnson School is. Although the school is on a busy North-South thoroughfare, there is no sign at the driveway to tell all passersby that this is "Johnson School." When I worked at Carter & Burgess, it drove me crazy that, although we were located on a busy highway, few people outside our business knew we were there. That's because the company posted its name on the orange brick building in four- or five-inch-high brass letters, instead of in huge, two-foot-high script.

3. **Revamp the communications program.** Johnson School puts out a monthly parent newsletter, but the newsletter lacks tangible measures of how the school is stacking up. We suggested including a monthly poll of parents, teachers, and students on how the school is doing. Another idea was to install a telephone answering machine that would let anyone call and give input, something else that could show up in the newsletter. The message for A/E/P and environmental firms: Internal communication is critical to the change process— especially when you can quantify your progress.

4. **Start a new public relations program.** Everyone needs to know that this is a "new Johnson School," if the school is to get the attention it needs to survive. The success of the all-day Kindergarten program, the fact that we have a new "businessman-turned-principal," and the widespread participation in the school's science fair must be promoted. And this promotion should occur throughout the local, and perhaps even national media (national media would give it even more credibility). I say it almost daily to our clients— take advantage of the free advertising you can get by an aggressive PR campaign.

Design or environmental firms who want their overhauls to be successful should take note of what's happening at Johnson School: you have to get the message out to *everybody* if you want the change to take hold. **Z**

D E T A I L S

GETTING INTO PRINT: In today's competitive market for architectural, engineering, and environmental consulting work, a spread in a magazine— especially one that reaches an audience of potential clients— can save thousands of marketing dollars and also capture the attention of clients.

Here are some tips for effective marketing:

■ *Publish original research.* That can mean an article authored by the firm's expert on a particular topic, a survey bearing the name of the firm, or an opinion piece from an expert in the firm. Publishing well thought out, original research gives the A/E/P or environmental consulting firm a tremendous advantage over its competitors because it instantly positions the firm as an expert on the topic.

■ *Create "stars" at the firm.* From the media's standpoint, "experts" don't necessarily have to be the most knowledgeable or experienced people in the firm. More often, they are simply those who are willing and able to communicate clearly with the media in a manner that contributes to a more interesting, informative, and entertaining story.

■ *Do pro-bono work.* Offer the firm's services free of charge on a project. One A/E firm that designed a homeless shelter found itself mentioned in the local papers, the national press, and on *CNN.*

■ *Encourage community and professional involvement.* Just because news isn't "big," doesn't mean it lacks publicity benefits. The more "little" news you make, the better— as long as it's favorable.

■

MARKETING in the professional services has come a long way— but not far enough. Once considered unprofessional, marketing is now an integral part of most A/E/P and environmental consulting firms. Nonetheless, based on the results of the *Marketing Survey of A/E/P & Environmental Consulting Firms* (Mark Zweig & Associates, March 1994), the industry still has a long way to go in perfecting the art of marketing.

For instance, *why* don't more firms make a real effort to build a list of every potential buyer of their services? You can't sell if you don't know who you're selling to!

Most firms maintain some kind of centralized database (or mailing list) of past, present, or potential clients— but these lists are *way* too small. According to the survey, the median firm's mailing list had only 33 names on it for every employee in the firm (names in list divided by number of employees).

Maybe one reason firms aren't building their lists is because they don't really believe in the power of direct mail. Direct mail is often considered the *least* successful marketing strategy that can be used. In our opinion, firms dismiss direct mail because they haven't gone about it the right way or else have set their expectations too high.

■

Evolution of marketing

SOMETIMES it's helpful to assess where you've come from before deciding where you want to go. This is certainly the case when it comes to marketing for the typical A/E or consulting engineering firm. Fortunately, most firms in this business have come a long way, although many still have a long way to go.

Following is the typical evolution of marketing in an A/E/P or consulting engineering firm (environmental consultants are excluded because they did not necessarily go through all the "bad" programming the rest of us in more traditional A/E firms got early-on in our careers):

Stage 1: Firm starts out working for people the principal personally knows. All work is done with handshake agreements. Client is sent the bill when the firm is through working. Firm takes any work it can get.

Stage 2: Firm puts the qualifications of the principal in writing— can provide to whoever needs it. Can do whatever client wants. After all, an engineer is an engineer, and an architect is an architect. Firm still takes all work at any fee.

Stage 3: Firm develops rudimentary brochure. Adds more principals in newer disciplines. Founder's secretary starts to handle typing of all proposals. Firm *still* takes practically all work at any fee.

Stage 4: Secretary is devoted full-time to marketing. Proposal documents become more refined. Firm develops standard project descriptions and résumés for professional staff, and generates standardized proposals.

Stage 5: Secretary joins SMPS and is now called *marketing coordinator*. Principals do all selling. Firm revises brochure and company logo. Prepares first SF255. Purchases business card ads in back of *ENR* and state professional association directories. Buys word processing system. If it's an engineering firm, it's now in position to turn down work from local architect who never pays his bills, yet still drives expensive European car. If it's an architectural firm, it can turn down the garage addition for the sleazy discount store chain owner's house.

Stage 6: Firm hires outside business development person from industry or government to sell big projects, which immediately causes disruption in the firm. Fires that person six months to a year later and hires second business development person. He or she, too, often fails. If not, firm takes person out of element by moving into in-house marketing director function.

Stage 7: Firm forms business development committee to make decisions on marketing— i.e. teaming, go/no-go, fees, etc. Names firm principal director of marketing. Hires experienced marketing coordinator away from another firm. Develops first primitive marketing plan. If it's an engineering firm, it makes the decision to move away from so much interprofessional work and pursue industrial clients, and may add in-house architecture. If it's an architectural firm, it becomes more selective about its clients and may begin to specialize in one or more client types. Firm develops first external newsletter. Finally organizes project photo/slides. Revises brochure because all the people in the old one are standing alongside 1968 Ford Falcons, have dated hairstyles, and silly ties and lapels.

Stage 8: Firm hires new marketing director from another firm after principal is put out to pasture. Marketing plan becomes integral part of strategic business plan. Adopts new marketing organization structure, with certain principals heading up business development efforts in specific market sectors. Converts all marketing information to database on PC network. Adds desk-top publishing equipment and specialist. Revises corporate newsletter. Creates a marketing information system so the firm actually knows what it's selling to whom and for how much, proposal hit rates, presentation hit rates, and so on. Overhauls graphic image of the firm (throws out the "earth tone" color scheme). Begins experimental marketing efforts with company-sponsored training programs, trade show participation, research and direct mail.

Although Stage 8 may be as good as we've seen it to date, by no means do we feel this is the ultimate evolution of the marketing function for an A/E or environmental firm. As an industry, we're getting better every day. **Z**

D E T A I L S

BETTER 255s: Want to win more federal work? Here are some easy ways you can improve your Standard Form 255 proposals, according to marketing consultant Nancy Usrey, president of Partners Usrey (Irving, TX) and author of *Insider's Guide to SF254/255 Preparation* (Mark Zweig & Associates, 1993).

■ Thoroughly read the project announcement. Break it out point-by-point and use that information in every aspect of your submittal. As you read the announcement, develop a list of questions. Call the contact person and ask your questions to learn more about what the client wants.

■ Make sure projects you list in Item 8 also appear on résumés in Item 7. This shows the client your team has the specific experience it will need.

■ In Item 10, talk about more than the background of the firm. Organize your discussion in the same order as the evaluation criteria, and make sure you discuss every point identified in the announcement.

■ Boldface, underline, or italicize relevant words in the résumés, projects and Item 10. Anything to help reviewers find information about your firm is a benefit.

■ Put your organization chart on the back of each page facing a résumé. Also, on the back of each page facing your project descriptions, use a matrix to compare elements of those projects to the one you're bidding for. This summarizes your team and experience in pictures.

■ Expand your list of 10 past projects to include a relevant description of each project, up to one page for each project. The one-page form in 255 packages barely provides enough room to list the title and location of each project.

■

GETTING THE FAX OUT: RMC Environmental Services (Spring City, PA), a 150-person environmental firm, is saving fax paper and simultaneously doing some effective marketing. The firm's fax cover sheets include a timely environmental news item that also highlights one of RMC's services.

The company began putting its news box on faxes about a year ago, Marketing Director Margaret O'Malley says, and the results have been encouraging. "We have the form in desktop publishing, so it takes very little time and no money," she says.

For example, while working on a water quality project with a large electric utility, RMC sent that company a fax cover sheet that included a news item about an unrelated air quality project RMC was involved in. The person who received the fax passed the note on to the utility's air quality department manager, and RMC recently had some promising discussions about working with that division of the company.

Because it is illegal to solicit sales by fax, the company keeps its news items "newsy."

■

Financial Manager vs. Accountant

Finance and accounting staff in architecture, engineering, and environmental consulting firms go under a lot of different titles— controller, financial manager, director of finance, administrative director, chief financial officer, and so on.

And you can't always tell from someone's title what they really do. We've seen CFOs who are simply glorified bookkeepers, and we've seen controllers who understand the business better than many principals.

When, as happens fairly often, we're asked by clients to recommend someone for a "financial manager" or "controller" opening, it's sometimes difficult to pin down exactly what sort of person they're looking for.

We've found there are two basic types of financial people in our business— one, which we'll call the *Financial Manager*, and a second, which we'll call the *Accountant*. Here are a few ways to tell which is which:

■ Financial Manager warns principals when cash flow crunch is two to three months away and something can still be done about it. Accountant tells principals there is a problem when next week's payroll can't be met.

■ Financial Manager tracks down busy principal and gets him to approve and sign invoices so they can go out on time. Accountant lets invoices sit for 30 days until principal is ready to discuss.

■ Financial Manager reviews expense reports and challenges needless or unauthorized expenses from project managers. Accountant processes expense checks and forwards to principal to be signed.

■ Financial Manager builds relationship with bankers and educates them about business of the firm; advises principals to increase credit line when firm doesn't need it now, but may soon. Accountant responds to last minute request for financial data from principals who must meet with banker because credit line is maxed out.

■ Financial Manager stays current on tax regulations and practices of other design and environmental firms and identifies ways to cut taxes. Accountant supplies year-end financial summary to CPA so he can calculate tax obligation.

■ Financial Manager zealously guards firm's financial resources; refuses to pay frivolous "documentation fee" to lease company. Accountant disburses money when requested; fills out lease application and cuts documentation fee check for principal to sign.

■ Financial Manager attends continuing education courses on Federal Acquisition Regulations and recommends that firm change accounting practices to avoid potential audit. Accountant helps unpack financial records from 1979 so DCAA auditors who have set up camp in the conference room can scrutinize.

■ Financial Manager understands what business the firm is in and knows how all the pieces of the firm fit together. Accountant looks at each piece of the firm in isolation and misses big picture.

■ Financial Manager usually earns salary on-par with senior technical professionals in the firm. Accountant usually earns salary at high end of secretarial/administrative scale.

The bottom line: Accountants are reactive— they report the past. Financial Managers are proactive— they change the future.

Design and environmental consulting firms do *need* people to process the paperwork and keep the score. Most of the "Accountants" we know work hard and really sweat the details. Their firms would be lost without them.

But anyone with the title "CFO" or "Financial Manager" must aspire to do more than just report what happened last month. And their employers, in turn, need to expect more in the way of financial *management* from their accounting staff— and then listen to their advice. ∎

D E T A I L S
. . . .

SAMPLE CHIEF FINANCIAL OFFICER (CFO) ROLE DESCRIPTION:

REPORTS TO:

President (or CEO/ Managing Partner)

POSITION REQUIREMENTS:

Must be driven to improve the cash flow, liquidity, return on equity, profitability, capitalization, and long-term viability of the firm. Should be system-oriented and have a strong internal service orientation. Must strive to continuously improve the firm's position across every tangible financial measure.

SUMMARY DESCRIPTION OF DUTIES AND RESPONSIBILITIES:

■ Overall mission is to make sure the company is able to survive, pay its bills promptly, and adequately reward stockholders through profits that can be extracted from the company as a result of operations and investments, and through longer-term growth in the value of their equity in the company.

■ Responsible for development of firm-wide budget and for alerting management to the problems and what to do about them when the firm is not meeting the budget.

■ Provides all managers in the firm with the information they need to manage projects, teams, departments, and offices.

■ Supervises all assigned finance and accounting support staff, which may include accounts payable, accounts receivable, payroll, contract review, etc.

■ Maintains and reports all financial statistics regarding the firm's performance, including cash flow, accrual P&L, and balance sheet.

■ Develops and maintains company-wide database of information on past projects/clients from a profitability and historical collections point of view.

■ Runs credit checks on all new clients through Dun & Bradstreet or other sources.

■ Assists principals, project managers, and office managers with collection of delinquent accounts.

■ Acts as firm's agent to negotiate banking/credit relationships.

■ Reviews contracts as required.

■ Manages company-owned real estate assets.

■ Makes lease/buy decisions on all new capital equipment.

■ Develops requirements for, implements, and maintains company-wide project cost accounting system.

■ Prepares and internally distributes information that bolsters financial victories and reinforces successful management efforts of individuals in the firm.

■ Provides training to technical/ professional staff in financial and accounting issues that affect them.

■ Manages and reports on viability of ownership transition program.

■

Fixing PM problems

VIRTUALLY *everyone* who owns or manages an A/E, consulting engineering, or environmental consulting firm is concerned about project management (PM). And most of these people are certain their firm's ability to manage jobs could improve.

Here are some typical project management problems, along with my recommendations for dealing with them:

1. **The PM system is not geared to handle small projects.** Most firms in this business have lots of small projects, as opposed to a few major ones that last a long time. I routinely see companies with as many as 300 people that have average project fees in the range of $10,000 or less. Yet, most have PM systems far too complex to handle these smaller jobs.

   Just about everything written on project management and training seems to be geared for the "mega-project." It's not unusual to get advice like "estimate every job three ways," "hold a kick-off meeting with all project team members," "hold review meetings at every stage," "do a full wall schedule," and so forth. This doesn't work when you have small jobs that are started and completed in a matter of days or weeks. Firms should analyze their entire PM process and remove every step they can.

2. **Too many phase, task and activity codes.** Engineers, in particular, want to make everything more scientific than it really is. We performed a management audit and orchestrated the assembly of a strategic business plan for a 20-person, single-discipline firm with two offices. They had two single-spaced pages of task, phase and activity codes, with over 25 non-billable activity codes, and more than 60 billable ones. So everyone hated doing time sheets (they were always late), the time they recorded was inaccurate, the project management reports were four or more pages long instead of one, and the critical data on how much money was left in the budget was hard to find. So the PMs didn't read the reports, and project profitability suffered. We cut it back to four non-billable activity codes and eight billable task codes. This made everything much simpler and the company more profitable.

3. **The PM role is not perceived as prestigious.** Too many firms make office manager and department head jobs the powerful ones, and de-emphasize the project management function. This is reinforced by the fact that in many firms, the PM has little or no real authority. As a result, the PM role is seen only as a stepping stone. And if that's the case, why do it too well? You'll just get stuck there! The PM role should be seen as one of the most important (if not the most important) in the company.

4. **The PM role is not clearly defined.** This is especially critical in terms of what the PM is responsible for, compared to the PIC, discipline heads, project engineer, or lead designer. This role confusion makes duplication of efforts and omissions possible. To solve this problem, every firm needs to develop clearly defined descriptions of responsibilities and degree of decision-making latitude for each member of the team.

5. **Most firms do little or no formal training of PMs, nor do they give preference to candidates with management education for new PM roles.** As a result, PM per-

formance is poor, particularly in the areas of supervising people and written and verbal communications. Technical people are often poor managers because they've never been exposed to the "science" of the subject. They're often poor writers because they've never been taught how. They learned the stilted and confused style from predecessors, who also weren't trained.

6. **Most firms do not reward good PMs more than mediocre ones.** Too many PMs are really "project processors" versus "results-affecters." They see themselves as administrators, not people who can really make a difference, and blame their woes on the client or on staff who don't report to them (which may, in fact, be a real problem). There's no question that PMs do have one of the toughest, if not *the* toughest, jobs in the typical A/E or environmental firm. To get and keep *good* project managers, firms have to pay them better than mediocre performers. We resist doing that, preferring instead to pass out across-the-board raises and bonuses based on position level, not performance or value to the firm. Then we take forever to cull the dead wood. So we systematically run off our best performers and keep our worst!

7. **Since most PMs come out of a technical or design discipline area, they often don't consider project management "real" work.** When pressed for an honest answer, many PMs admit this *is* how they feel. The result of this thinking is they devote their time to technical tasks and ignore the responsibilities of the PM role. This *has* to affect the quality of project management. The problem is exacerbated by bosses who also came from technical backgrounds. To change this attitude, top management *must* sell PMs on the importance of their roles.

Problems with project management will always be with us. But it's time we started dealing with the *controllable* variables in the PM equation so we can be better prepared for all the *uncontrollable* ones. **z**

D E T A I L S

TOO OFTEN, design and environmental consulting firms initiate a performance appraisal or incentive compensation system based on hard numbers, only to keep the actual numbers a secret from those who are being appraised. As a result, staffers have no way of knowing how they're doing or how to adjust their performance.

Once while visiting 200-person E/A firm Shive-Hattery Engineers-Architects, Inc. (Cedar Rapids, IA), to give a presentation on marketing for their project managers, we watched a powerful testimony to the motivational power of basic communication.

Shive-Hattery had been highly profitable. Firm president David Johnson wouldn't say precisely *how* profitable, but admitted that people had been pretty happy. What was Shive-Hattery doing right?

The performance of project managers at Shive-Hattery is tracked three ways: by gross fees billed, by budget variance in dollars, and by percentage budget variance. PMs at Shive-Hattery typically sell the work they manage, so gross fees are an indicator of sales activity and project workload.

Bonuses for PMs are based on a combination of factors, including effort (as measured in the number of hours over 40 per week they work), amount of work managed, and several "soft" factors taken from ratings by top management.

In the past, Johnson had been tracking these numbers by quar-

ters and putting them up on a bulletin board for all to see. One day, however, he decided, "with a certain amount of fear and trepidation," to publicly honor those people who had improved the most.

At the annual PM meeting, Executive Vice President Tom Hayden outlined new criteria for being considered a "top project manager" at Shive-Hattery. Then, one by one, he put the 12 top PM's performance stats on the screen.

Starting with the top-ranked PM, he worked his way down the list, discussing the achievements of each individual. Hayden also reviewed the performance of the person who *climbed* the most places in that year's ratings compared with the previous year, as well as the person who *fell* the most places over the past year.

"The human motivation people will tell you that there's no more powerful motivator than recognition in front of your peers," says Johnson. "After that meeting, I asked managers what they thought of it. The people who were the heroes really appreciated it. The people who didn't make it said, 'I'm going to be up there next time.'"

The system must be working, as the firm has a very high percentage of repeat clients and a strong backlog of work.

◼

Generation "X"

WHILE WAITING to catch a plane from Philadelphia to Boston the other day, I stood in line for what seemed like the longest time with a group of college students heading home for the Easter weekend. I then ended up sitting next to them in the departure lounge.

I could not help overhearing a conversation between one young fellow and a young woman. Both were about 21, clean cut, and they obviously knew each other. They were talking about career choices, something I have always been interested in.

The young man told the young woman he had his career all mapped out. "Yeah," he said. "I'm going into civil engineering because doctors don't really make that much." I thought to myself, "Only about $135,000 per year compared to $60,000 for an equally experienced civil engineer."

"I'm going to work on the Central Artery project for four years, then get my MBA," he continued. "I'll never have to do any engineering from that point forward."

Right then, I felt like stepping in and telling this kid that it was pretty unlikely, even if he had his MBA, that he would be able to get completely out of engineering with only four years of experience. But before I could say anything, the conversation continued.

The young woman said: "I'm not really, like, sure what I want to, like, do yet. I thought, like, about accounting, but I'm not really, like, sure." Listening to her talk was like hearing the proverbial fingernails on the blackboard. "Where in the world do all of those 'likes' come from?" I wondered to myself. It was painful listening to her.

Then came the lad's response to all this: "Yeah," he said. "Accounting is okay, except for the fact that the first three years all you do is make 150 phone calls a day."

"*What* is this guy talking about?" I thought to myself. "150 phone calls a *day*— in accounting? He must have an entry-level accountant confused with a stockbroker trainee."

Finally, after 150 more "likes" from the girl, and another half-dozen career misconceptions from the guy, I got on my plane. Fortunately, we were not seated near each other, so I didn't hear any more of their chatter. But after reflecting on it for a few days, some thoughts came to me:

1. **A/E/P and environmental firms should hire co-op students and interns for entry-level positions instead of hiring new graduates who have never set foot inside a firm in this industry.** The career guidance young people get must be terrible if the kind of misconceptions I overheard the other day are in any way typical. Misconceptions lead to disappointment. Disappointment leads to a search for a new job. Co-ops and interns are much more likely to stay with you over the long haul because they know what to expect.

2. **We really have to work hard to make sure expectations for our younger employees are realistic.** For example, if someone says that once he has an MBA he doesn't plan to do any more real work, we need to tell him the truth. Very few people get out of technical work only four years into their career in the A/E/P and environmental consulting business, MBA or not. And if that did happen, it would probably be terrible for them in the long-term. But if that is their expectation, is it any wonder these people

usually only last a couple of years on the job? Let's be straight with them.

3. **There is a crying need for training in communications skills, especially for young people.** Weaned on Nintendo, many of the "Generation X'ers" I know never read a book unless they have to. Their speech mannerisms come straight out of "Wayne's World" and MTV. I would be totally embarrassed if we had a twenty-something employee who inserted "like" into every sentence and that person ever came into contact with one of our clients. Yet, these people must be getting jobs somewhere! **z**

D E T A I L S

· · · · · · · · · · · · · · · · · · · ·

IF YOU wonder whether college co-op programs work, talk to Fred Donovan, president of 100-person A/E firm Baskerville-Donovan Engineers, Inc. (Pensacola, FL). About one-tenth of his firm's employees came from its co-op program.

Morris Clark began working for the firm as a co-op student from Auburn University 26 years ago. He's now a senior civil engineer. "Co-op programs can be a win-win-win situation. If you get a properly motivated, smart, ready-to-learn student, the school wins, the student wins, and the company wins," says Donovan.

Deanna Moore, assistant director for cooperative education at Louisiana State University, agrees. "From the company's point of view, it's a real recruitment tool, because they can hire students ahead of the competition," she says. "It also gets work performed almost at the level of a professional engineer, but for far less."

George Frost could also tell you a successful co-op story— his own. The president of Rist-Frost Associates, P.C. (Glens Falls, NY), a 60-person consulting engineering firm, Frost is a 1950 graduate of Boston's Northeastern University. Upon graduation, Frost was hired by a client of his co-op employer. "If it weren't for the co-op program, I wouldn't be where I am now," says Frost. "That's how I paid my way through school."

Here's how to make a college co-op program work:

Make sure the work is challenging. Frost dropped his firm's co-op program when he ran out of challenging work for the students. "You can't just let them be a gofer making prints. It's terrible to do that," he says.

Educate managers and other staffers why you're establishing a co-op program. "To start a successful co-op program, you have to be organized, and upper management has to be pro-active in deciding where it's going to use the student and who is going to be the student's mentor," says Moore.

Develop a pay scale and provide the information to potential co-op students and to the school. The co-op students in the engineering school at LSU make an average of $1,500-$2,000 a month. But Moore says that is higher than average because most of the school's co-op companies are Fortune 500 firms.

Keep the co-op position continuously staffed. Your professional staff is only going to use co-ops as a resource if they *know* there's always going to be someone in the position.

Don't give up during bad times. "You can't make a co-op program part of overhead— it has to be part of production. If it's going to be part of overhead, even in good times, don't do it. Part of the professional staff's payment is based on profit, and if co-op students aren't adding something, they'll look at those kids as if they're taking money out of their pockets," says Donovan.

■

Getting extra effort in good times

I T'S A RARE A/E or environmental consulting firm that didn't have some lean months during the recession of the early 1990s. Even if they didn't lay off anyone, most principals have on occasion asked employees to dig in and work a little harder to get through a slow period.

Now many of these same firms are thriving and facing a new problem— complacency. The trouble is that while it's fairly easy to get on your soapbox and rally the troops when the firm is in a crisis (impending doom *does* create a sense of urgency), it's much harder to motivate people in good times.

Don't quit while you're ahead. Overcoming adversity, making big gains, and then seeing them swallowed back up because the firm coasts for a few months is a major cause of *burnout* among firm principals. Now it's the things you *do*, not what you *say*, that will push the firm on to the next level of prosperity:

1. **Set higher goals.** When the firm does well, everyone may feel they deserve a pat on the back. It's time to re-evaluate the old goals and push them higher.

2. **Hire people who want to achieve more.** Ron Daniel, the former managing director of McKinsey & Co. (New York, NY), the big management consulting firm, has an un-

usual approach in this area: "We look to hire people who are, first, very smart; second, insecure, and thus driven by their insecurity; and, third, competitive." Too many people in design and environmental consulting firms have already *exceeded* their personal goals. Prosperity is a good time to upgrade your staff with smart, hungry people.

3. **Bring in more owners.** Who's usually the first one in and/or the last one out of your firm every day? Who's most likely to be found at their desks on Saturday or Sunday? Nothing gets more effort out of most professionals than owning a piece of the firm. And good times are the right time to consider bringing in new stockholders— the firm's value is high and profits are there to fund the buy-in.

4. **Confront people problems creatively.** It's easy to rationalize letting things slide when the firm is successful. But problem people in key positions can put a real drag on your efforts to push the firm to a higher level. If someone failed when the firm was on a smaller scale, how is he or she going to make it on the next level? On the other hand, growth creates new and different jobs, one of which may be better matched to a problem employee. Richard A. Smith, president of R.A. Smith & Associates (Brookfield, WI), a 75-person consulting engineering firm, says his firm will often change an employee's work environment in an effort to improve job performance and satisfaction. Be creative and you may create a new star just by changing the role.

5. **Be willing to re-invest, not just reap.** Success puts a strain on your infrastructure. This can trigger an orgy of hiring, reorganizing, office expansions, capital expenditures, and so on. Investment comes hard for many risk-averse design and environmental firm principals. But the alternative— asking staff to share desks, wait in line to use a computer, and work 60 hours a week for months on end— is bound to erode morale.

While you're at it, *training* is a good way to re-invest. Tom Veratti, founder of CON-TEST, Inc. (East Longmeadow, MA), an environmental consulting firm that grew from one to 180 employees in just a few years, has learned to devote time and money to training.

6. **Share the rewards.** Times were tough last year and you asked Joe the project manager to hang on for another year to get his raise. So give it to him now. People must believe they have an incentive to push on to higher goals. Promises only work so long. Give key people tangible evidence of your generosity.

   Look at Robert Stude, vice president and treasurer of consulting engineers Boyd, Brown, Stude & Cambern (Kansas City, MO). He says a new bonus plan tied to profitability offered to employees about a year ago helped *boost* profits and spurred growth from 40 to 60 employees. And engineers are more satisfied with their work because they can see it paying off.

7. **Keep people informed.** Just because you're busy doesn't mean you're rolling in *cash*. If you're growing, it's probably the opposite. Make sure your people understand this. A staff that's kept apprised of the firm's performance knows when there's extra money to go around and when there isn't, says Paul Cropsey, a principal at Cropsey, Upson & Associates (Griffin, GA), a seven-person A/E firm.

8. **Finally, in your zeal to motivate people, resist over- investing and over-rewarding.** We've seen many firms overextend themselves and give away the store, especially in terms of compensation and benefits, after a good year or two. **Z**

D E T A I L S

IT'S BEEN SAID before that "the seeds of destruction are sown along with your success." In my experience, there's truth to that old adage when it's applied to A/E/P and environmental consulting firms. Many companies in this business don't handle success very well, and as a result, destroy their future opportunities in the process.

Here are some of the things firms who are currently successful should be aware of:

■ Overtime policies. I have seen this time and time again. Instead of spending the time to create and implement a well thought-out bonus program, firms with staffs that are highly billable somehow get the idea that to be fair to their exempt employees they have to start paying them overtime. This practice encourages and rewards inefficiency.

■ Extravagance. For many firms, when times are good, the corporate Buicks turn into corporate BMWs; lunch at Red Lobster becomes lunch at "Marios"; every principal hires his own private secretary; and the CEO trades in his 200 square foot office for an 800 square foot one. Lo and behold, overhead creeps up to the point where profitability becomes almost an impossibility.

■ Investments in assets that don't make money but instead cost money to maintain. A classic example of this is the company office building. Even worse is the company vacation retreat or the company yacht. I won't argue that sometimes these things can be good investments, but more often,

they become anchors that pull your head under water when the first wave rolls in.

■ Lack of investments in what is making money. It's always interesting to me to see companies that are doing well in one office, or in one technical specialty area, and then act like they are spending their last dollar when it comes time to hire someone or make a small acquisition that would increase their capacity to serve that market. We have a very hard time distinguishing between what is really risky because it's purely speculative and what we know we can make money doing.

■ Assumptions that the good times will last forever. This kind of thinking is usually at the core of the problems listed above, yet it's completely baffling. Good times don't last forever. They never have and they never will. After every boom there will be a bust. At the bottom of every crest is a trough. That's the way it is. Yet when a firm is on an extended roll, it's not unusual for management/ownership to become complacent and arrogant. The assumption is that all of the company's success is due to their own wisdom— and that can be dangerous.

■

Getting organized

OUR MANAGEMENT consulting work for A/E/P and environmental consulting firms frequently gets us into the area of organization structure. It seems no matter what you want to change, the structure always becomes an issue.

There are professional and technical people working in firms who, when the subject of organization structure comes up, say: "Oh yeah— it's been a year now. It's time to change the organization structure again so we can give all those overhead people something to waste time with."

While I'd love to say that every time an organization structure changes, it's for the better, I'm not that naïve. I realize a lot of bad things have been done to organization structures in A/E/P and environmental firms because I have had the opportunity to undo many of those structures. Here are some organization structure trouble spots:

1. **Directors of QA/QC.** I've been harping on this one for years, but I still see individuals listed on corporate organization charts as the QA/QC Director. And with very few exceptions, the story is the same. That's the guy no one thought could manage a department or office, run a project, or sell work, so they created a slot for him.

2. **Directors of Special Projects.** This is another job that is always a red flag to me, something worthy of scrutiny. Most of the time it is again a slot created to fit a person who doesn't fit in.

3. **Committees running the firm.** Why are so many professional practices— particularly architectural firms— set up with everyone reporting to an operating committee of some sort? I'm convinced it's either because no one wants to assume control or they think this set-up is somehow more egalitarian. The problem is that it violates a principle from "Management 101" called "unity of command"— every individual reports to one, and only one, boss.

4. **Rotational positions for the president, CEO, or treasurer.** This practice has two forms. One involves sharing the jobs between principals because no one really wants any management role permanently. The other occurs when the principals have a CFO, marketing director, etc., yet refuse to give that person any authority by appointing an owner as the ultimate authority. They then take turns as the staffer's tormentor.

5. **Multi-partner reporting.** I've seen a number of situations where, instead of a CEO, there are two equal partners everyone ultimately reports to. This doesn't work. We have an old saying in our business— "Shared responsibility means no responsibility."

6. **Partners or owners filling all management roles.** As an owner, I want to avoid as much of the day-to-day management as I can. The day I'm no longer managing people will be the day I know I have really made it.

7. **Partners not reporting to anyone.** This is fairly typical, but too much of this nonsense and a firm ends up in chaos. Everyone has to have a boss. They have to be accountable to someone.

8. **Associates who come from all over the company but really don't have a clear-cut role.** In the A/E and environ-

mental consulting business, we love to give out the title "Associate." But while at Circuit City the other day, I noticed that my salesperson's name tag said "Associate." If that title doesn't mean higher pay, more benefits or greater status, why have it?

9. **Pooled CADD.** Drafting pools for most of what we do in this business do not work. They reduce learning opportunities for CADD operators and professionals alike. They do not lead to higher quality. No one who is really any good wants to work in a pool. They want to be on a *team*. And the same goes for pooled word processing.

10. **Strict discipline departments.** Discipline departments are fine when technology is driving everything, such as seismic design, or indoor air quality. They don't work as well in mature service areas where knowledge of the discipline is widely available and assumed by the client. In those cases, it's knowledge of the client type that's important, and the structure should reflect that.

11. **Geographic-based structures.** I never understood this, yet I see large firms do it all of the time. They have divisions based on region. But does everyone in the Northeast want the same thing out of an A/E firm? Of course not— that's why this structure makes no sense. It also sets up a potential conflict on who goes after what job where.

12. **Titles like "Senior Executive VP."** I saw that in a newsletter from a prominent firm recently. All this does is make the company look silly. What kind of organization do you think of when you see everyone with a lofty title— banks, right? And banks aren't exactly paragons of efficiency. So why model ourselves after them? **Z**

D E T A I L S

• • • • • • • • • • • • • • • • •

IT'S NO SECRET. I really like standing team organization structures. Sometimes these team structures are also called "studios." But no matter what they are called, they share certain common elements:

■ *Restricted size.* The ideal team is probably about 8 people. More than 10 or 12, and the span of control gets too great. Less than 5 or 6, and there may not be the right mix.

■ *A single leader.* Teams are headed up by a principal or manager who is the clearly established leader. There's no ambiguity in determining who is whose boss in a structure that uses standing teams.

■ Longer-term working relationships. People in a team are constantly being shuffled off here or there, to work on any number of different teams during the week or the month. As a result, these people tend to learn each other's strengths and weaknesses, and more consistently put out a better quality product.

Assuming a firm is sold on the benefits of a standing team or studio structure, and puts one in place, what are some ways to make sure it all works?

1. Put the team members together in one place. This may mean you have to move some desks or even walls, but it's well worth it. People who work closely together enjoy better communication.

2. Count the beans by team. This means that you should count sales, revenues, and even profits by team, as opposed to only looking at offices or projects. This helps the

team form an identity and makes it possible for them to set quantifiable goals, something that is essential for them to pull together.

3. Have a good team leader. This means more than technical competence, it also requires leadership and communication abilities. This means you have to invest in training your team leaders. It also means those who fail despite coaching from more senior management may need to be moved into another position or out of the firm.

4. *Reward team performance.* Rewards are critical to reinforce what management wants its employees to do, yet all too often, rewards in A/E/P firms are doled out based on seniority, status in the pecking order, or how the firm does overall, and team performance is never recognized in any tangible way.

■

QUOTABLE: "Too many people have hired someone in the organization as CEO because they're there and everybody is comfortable with them, rather than stepping back and assessing the individual's real capabilities. They end up getting a clone of everybody who's there, with the same lack of vision, and lack of management and leadership skills. I can see them sitting around saying, 'We need a CEO. Let's have Joe do it.' That leads to a lot of disappointments."

SOURCE: John Benz, CEO at Tilden, Lobnitz & Cooper, Inc. (Orlando, FL), a 110-person engineering and architecture firm.

■

Healthy self-image

'VE ALWAYS been a student of human interaction. So when I hear someone say of another person in a derogatory tone, "That Wilson sure has a big ego," I immediately ask myself, "Who is this guy to say Wilson has a big ego? Is he jealous because Wilson is more successful than he is?"

If Wilson is *less* successful than the speaker, I'm probably more inclined to listen. If, on the other hand, Wilson has racked up some impressive accomplishments, I might give *him* the benefit of the doubt.

I'm sure in the past I have been accused of having a big ego, so I'm bound to be sympathetic. But I'd like to think I'm more rational than that. I guess I have always believed that in order to be successful, you have to have a healthy self-image. If you can't see yourself as successful, how will anyone else? You have to be able to visualize yourself getting that new project, getting that promotion, or solving that tricky problem. In other words— as someone *deserving* of success.

Undoubtedly, there are people out there working at the highest levels in A/E and environmental consulting firms who others commonly say have "a big ego." In fact, despite appearances, the complete opposite might be true. These people may instead have some deep-seated insecurities they mask with a veneer of success.

As a leader in your firm, it's important to distinguish the pretenders from those with a healthy self-image. You want to hire the latter, because all factors being equal, they will probably be more successful. And, whether we're talking about a peer, an employee, or a client, it's important to distinguish between those who have a positive self-image and those who only *appear* to. Because it will affect just about every interaction you have with them.

There are ways to identify these "impersonators" by digging just a little below the surface. Here are some signs:

1. **Impersonators are much more concerned about the trappings of success than the intrinsic rewards that come from it.** Fancy cars, lavish houses, pricey clothes, lofty titles, and short-term income are more important to these people than long-term income, the value of their equity in their firm, and the satisfaction that comes from being a team player in building a successful business. The reason is, deep down, big ego impersonators fear they could be exposed at some point and lose everything. So their attitude is: "Better get it now because who knows what tomorrow will bring."

2. **Impersonators have a history of sour relations with other people.** They aren't willing to risk rejection or failure in a personal relationship, so they never invest the time and emotional energy to form one that's more than superficial. As principals, impersonators tend to blame others for their failure— their staff is never good enough. They are down on others because they have a negative view of themselves.

3. **Impersonators can often only perform in one narrow band of knowledge and fail once they get out of that.** Whether it's a narrowly defined managerial role or a single technical specialty area, the impersonator is distinguished from the real thing by his complete lack of flexibility. The biggest problem may not be innate ability— it's an unwillingness to try anything that really tests their

capabilities for fear of being exposed as failures (and, in their minds, frauds).

4. **Impersonators cannot visualize anything that's too abstract.** If a future scenario is too far removed from their own experience, the big ego impersonators will see it as "B.S." These people will almost always oppose any changes in the company that require an investment and don't have an immediate pay-off— things like implementing a strong human resources department, or establishing an on-line project management control system, or investing in a P.C. for everyone's desk.

5. **Impersonators often tell "white lies" or practice other petty acts of dishonesty.** People with a poor self-image often lie to boost others' opinion of them. They'll lie about how much money they make, how much of the company's stock they own, their family background, or what their spouse does for a living, many times for no apparent reason.

Taking the time to study the behavior or your staff, peers and clients is time well-spent for anyone in a leadership role in an A/E/P or environmental consulting firm. You can't always tell who has a good self-image and who has a poor one by a first impression. But it's important to you as a manager and consultant to find out. **Z**

D E T A I L S

· · · · · · · · · · · · · · · · · · · ·

I WAS TALKING recently with a labor relations lawyer about the issue of sexual harassment and its effect on employer-employee relations. He told me about some situations his non-consulting clients encountered that illustrate the far reaches of this issue and highlight questions of an employer's level of responsibility.

In one case, a secretary observed, through an open door, another secretary in the embrace of the latter's boss. The first secretary reported what she saw to management. Upon questioning, the accused manager explained that his assistant had just experienced a family tragedy, and he was comforting her. The assistant corroborated the story and defended her boss, but the company "wrote up" the guy anyway.

In another story, a CEO was accused by a female employee of creating an environment conducive to sexual harassment. The CEO, a woman who is an avid art collector, kept several sculptures in the building's lobby, including some of partially clothed female figures.

I also spoke recently with the HR manager of an A/E firm who was handling a complaint from a staffer who reported being harassed by one of the firm's sub-consultants at a site meeting. It's very important that the A/E employer apply its own procedures to the matter. Not only will it be more prepared for possible legal repercussions, but, perhaps more importantly, will provide critical support to its employee.

RETIREMENT REQUIREMENT: Dick Fruth, a partner at 105-person E/A firm Hayes Large Architects (Altoona, PA), has no problem with the firm's mandatory retirement policy for principals. "I plan to be out by 62," says Fruth. "I want to enjoy my retirement."

Fruth strongly supports the rule. "The thought is, 'Look, you have a definite time to get out, so plan your finances accordingly.' The key thing is getting a person out right after they've peaked, and not allowing them to stay on for years and years," he says.

Fruth says the 72-year-old firm established the policy in the 1950s after a partner lingered long past 65 and was unproductive. He says the firm's lawyers say the policy is not discriminatory because every partner agrees to it in writing.

Not everyone likes the idea. Becky Braman, president of Intermountain Professional Services, Inc. (Cheyenne, WY), a 10-person consulting engineering firm, is one who opposes mandatory retirement. Braman says each situation should be judged individually. "Some people are still active into their 80s," she says. "Others lose interest in their 40s."

Marty Dirks, president of 150-person E/A firm KCM, Inc. (Seattle, WA), agrees. "I don't think being unproductive is a geriatrics issue," he says. "At least from what I've seen, that's not the main problem. This can hit any of us at any time."

Hire slowly and fire quickly

WITH THE economic rebound underway, firms are naturally starting to staff up. There are a lot of design firms out there who've put off hiring just about as long as they can— particularly traditional architecture, A/E, and engineering firms. And we're hearing from an increasing number of recruiters lately, as well as firms that need recruiting help.

This is good news for job-hunting engineers and architects, but not necessarily for their employers. Over the last few years many firms have learned how to be profitable by getting the most from a lean, experienced staff. They've shed the deadwood and developed the new stars. Now they have to remember how to staff up. They have to take another gamble on interviewing, hiring, training, and trying to integrate new people. And they have to do it in an employment market that's quickly heating up, where the best people have multiple options.

The most oft-repeated advice about hiring and firing sounds good on the surface: "Hire slowly and fire quickly." In other words, do your homework before you hire so you'll make a smarter choice. Then, if and when you *do* make a hiring blunder, don't prolong the agony. However, while it makes sense in theory, this advice is hard for the typical design or environmental firm to actually put into practice.

In fact, most of us do the exact opposite— we hire quickly and we fire slowly. And it's not because we're stupid and don't learn from our mistakes. There are some very good reasons:

Firms often have no choice but to hire quickly. They must put off hiring as long as possible to maintain high utilization. Then one new project may be enough to push production capacity beyond the breaking point. It's hire someone or miss a deadline. Hire someone or lose a project. In other cases, a key staffer quits suddenly, leaving a void that must be filled immediately. Firms in this position don't have the luxury of conducting four interviews with a candidate and negotiating for three months.

On the other hand, firms have many dis-incentives to firing quickly. For one, most engineers and architects don't like having to fire people. Confrontations can get messy. Also, firings may be bad for morale— even if the person fired is unpopular, it can create unease throughout the staff. There is also the specter of a wrongful termination suit, particularly (but not only) in the case of women, minorities, and people over age 40.

The real wisdom in the advice to hire slowly and fire quickly is not to *prolong* the hiring process unnecessarily or to keep a *hair trigger* on your termination process. The moral is to *always* be recruiting and to *always* be identifying and trying to rehabilitate problem employees— regardless of any immediate plans to hire or fire.

By maintaining a consistent recruiting effort in good times and bad, you'll have the benefits of a "slow," thorough hiring process, yet be able to move quickly when you need to. By constantly grooming and farming your staff for potential morale and performance problems, you'll be able to spot trouble earlier and do your best to turn it around, while delivering and documenting the warnings that will make you comfortable with firing an employee if there is no other choice.

As firms begin to grow again this year, there are plenty of opportunities to make *bad* hires because you're in a hurry— hires that will turn into the firings of the future. Why not start your slow hiring process now? And meanwhile, start confronting problem employees and laying the legal and moral groundwork for any firings that lie down the road— you may even salvage some good people while you're at it. ▪

D E T A I L S
• • • • • • • • • • • • • • • • • •

PROFESSIONAL service firms value low staff turnover. The sentiment is, "We're a people business, so we keep our people."

But more important than retention for retention's sake is "Who are we keeping and why?" In the same way we target-market and target-recruit, why can't we "target-retain"?

The first step is an ongoing staff performance evaluation process tied to a firm's overall business plan. This will identify firm-staff relationships that are no longer productive— or heading in that direction. Of course, the clearer a firm's short- and long-term plans are, the simpler it is to assess staff "fit." Why not try the following?

■ In pre-employment interviews with staff at all levels, make clear the goals and objectives of the firm's business plan, where individuals' roles fit in, and their expected contribution. Once hired, staff should know this discussion is the basis of evaluations.

■ As firm objectives change, identify conflicts and mismatches. For example, a project manager unwilling to undergo training when all PMs need to be CADD-proficient; a principal whose activities no longer justify his or her salary; or a municipal wastewater engineer in a firm that decides not to pursue those projects.

■ Work to rectify a staff mismatch by examining with the employee other firm roles that take advantage of his or her capabilities. If possible, provide cross-training (i.e., involve the wastewater engineer in other environmental projects). Moni-

tor that person's effectiveness in a new role.

When the options of re-positioning and training run out, it's better to let an employee go. Prolonging the employment of someone whose work doesn't serve the firm's objectives de-motivates employees whose efforts do. "Target-retention," like target-marketing, is an intentional, rather than haphazard, effort to achieve business planning goals.

■

ANOTHER AWARD-WINNING RESUME: Paul Burgess, president of Atlantic Environmental Services (Colchester, CT), sent us this résumé, which he received in response to a recent employment ad his firm placed.

The applicant claims to be a U.S. Army General and a Sheikh of Bahrain, with an I.Q. of 228, a bachelor's degree, master's degree, and five PhD's (not counting the National College of War). His résumé details job experience from paper boy and summer camp counselor to U.S. General to his current position as a fast-food worker. He has to his credit 638 inventions, 160 technical papers, seven technology texts, and 1,002 patents. "Please respond in writing because I do not have a telephone at this time," the cover letter says.

According to Burgess, this individual routinely sends different résumés to Atlantic when the firm runs an ad.

■

Internal transition

I N SPITE of the increased interest and activity in mergers and acquisitions, internal ownership transition is *still* the most common way for existing owners of A/E and environmental consulting firms to cash out. And with just a little planning and forethought, many of the common internal ownership transition pitfalls *can* be avoided:

- **Start now.** It's never too early to begin thinking about ownership transition. What are your ultimate goals for the value of your equity? It's amazing to me how many principals can't even answer that question. Many have told me that they simply never thought about their ownership in those terms. They don't realize that ownership in a professional services firm *can* be worth something significant. No wonder so many seem to have a hard time getting out with anything.

- **Reduce the share of ownership that any one person holds.** Too much ownership in the hands of any one principal almost always creates a "Catch-22" for internal transition. If the company *isn't* profitable, it can't afford to pay people enough to buy the stock. If it *is* profitable, the stock is probably worth so much that no one can *afford* to buy it.

- **Spread out the ownership to people in different age brackets.** Several of our clients (firms with between 200 and 700 employees) are in the position where more than 40% of their existing ownership will be leaving the firm over a single three-year period. The effect of having all principals in the same age group is the same as having too much stock held by one person— it's a barrier to transition.

- **Have a buy/sell agreement that clearly specifies how the value of the stock is established.** Thank goodness most firms have this these days. But there are still companies that leave this issue up in the air until the time a stockholder leaves on his own or is let go. The lack of a valuation method in the buy-sell typically leads to widespread differences in the expectations of those parties at the buying and selling end, resulting in potentially costly internal conflicts, and in some cases, lawsuits.

- **Have an incentive compensation system that rewards percentage of ownership.** This is critical if you want to encourage individual owners to buy more stock. Too many companies have systems that result in the privileges of ownership being the same for those that own 2% as those that own 20%. I don't think it's fair, and it completely eliminates the incentive for the 2% shareholder to buy more stock. The result might be that when the 20% shareholder needs to get out, ten people have to replace him in the ownership structure. You then have the perks and bonus requirement of ten principals whereas before you had the perks and bonus of only one to contend with, not to mention the fact that ten people probably expect to be more involved in management now that they have become owners.

■ **Get life insurance for key principals.** Mark Zweig & Associates is now dealing with the sale of a company to its employees, a sale forced by the death of the firm's sole proprietor. Had the proprietor funded a life insurance program years ago with the *company* as the beneficiary, the firm would have had the money to buy out the widow immediately instead of needing as long as eight years to do it.

■ **Make sure that those who will take over the firm's management have the interest and the ability to do so.** Let's face it— ownership and management *are* tied together in the typical A/E or environmental consulting firm. Make sure that those who become owners have an interest in and aptitude for *business*. Make sure that new owners bring something new to the firm— such as the ability to get new work (that's number one for most professional service firms) or an ability to manage.

■ **Make sure that there is a clearly established management transition plan so that if someone dies or departs, a successor has already been decided.** This is necessary to avoid the costly internal turmoil that can result when a key person leaves the firm. It will also provide continuity to the management of the company. To do this properly, successors should be trained and ready to go as much as is possible.

■ **Get qualified outside advisors.** Too many times we have had to deal with business brokers, accountants, and attorneys who are not specialized in *our* business. They don't understand what's normal and give their clients a lot of bad advice. There *are* good advisors out there, but just like your clients select your firm over another because you have "done it before," you should do the same for ownership transition. **Z**

D   E   T   A   I   L   S

MERGING SALARIES AND BENEFITS: How do you deal with discrepancies in salaries and benefits between two partners in a merger?

The problem is particularly difficult if the higher earners come from the *selling* firm. "It's pretty hard to come in and cut salaries," says Frank T. Callahan, chairman and CEO at Greiner Engineering, Inc. (Irving, TX). "You either have to raise the level on one side, or accept the inequities and wait for them to even out over time."

Lawrence E. Newhart, Jr., president of Day & Zimmerman, Inc. (Philadelphia, PA), says he *has* cut salaries at acquired firms, but offered incentive packages that gave employees a chance to make *more* than they were making before.

"From a practical standpoint, the big dog rules," says Tim Lowe, executive vice president at Rosser Fabrap International (Atlanta, GA). "But if you want an acquisition to work in the long term, you have to even things out in a more gingerly fashion."

Principals should determine *before* the deal is made how much they need to move salaries and benefits toward middle ground— and how much employees on both ends will take before bailing out.

■

WHY DO *lawyers* make it so *hard* to make a deal? Rich Hangen, president at Vanasse Hangen Brustlin, Inc. (Watertown, MA), a 350-person consulting engineering firm, thought he was close to acquiring a seven-person pavement manage-ment company a few years ago. Then the lawyers showed up.

"We did the negotiations all the way without lawyers," Hangen says. "But when we started putting stuff down in writing, the attorneys started negotiating themselves and it created more problems than it solved."

The result— it took nearly 18 months to complete the deal. Hangen says a member of the acquired firm later told him their lawyers consistently advised against the transaction. It turned out a success for both companies, Hangen says, and all seven members of the acquired firm are still with his company.

Chris Thompson, president of Trow Consulting Engineers Ltd. (Brampton, ON), a 400-person firm, advises keeping lawyers out of the process as long as possible, no matter how large the acquisition. "They can scare the daylights out of you," he says.

Perhaps the problem is that too many lawyers don't feel they've earned their fees unless they extract something out of your counterpart in the negotiations. In some cases, this sort of wrangling gets your merger off on the wrong foot. In other cases, the lawyer isn't really getting you anything— as one principal says, "It costs me $500 in legal time for a $200 concession."

■

Is your house in order?

EVER BEEN house hunting? No matter what you can afford, it's never enough. Especially with the appalling things some people do to their homes.

I'm not just talking about starter homes (here in Boston, that's loosely defined as anything under a quarter-million dollars!)— I've seen plenty of expensive houses that look as if the owners had done absolutely no planning for how they would be used or decorated. They deal with each room in isolation of the others. An eight-room house might have seven kinds of carpeting. Some woodwork may be painted and some stained (in the same room). Colonial-style hardware is hung on contemporary kitchen cabinets.

Then there's stuff like 10-foot high bushes planted 12 inches from the foundation. Or three upstairs bedrooms sharing a half-bath, while downstairs has one bedroom and two baths. Or furniture placed like the obstacles on a miniature golf course. I could go on, but you get the idea— the people who own these houses had no grand scheme— no master plan to follow as they made improvements over the years. Houses end up like this because the owners' needs change and they just react.

Too many of us approach the development and growth of our businesses the same way we deal with our houses. We don't plan or think about where we want to go. Then, as the internal and external conditions change, we react to the latest demand or crisis. As a result, we sometimes end up with a firm that is vastly different from the one we originally set out to build.

That's why I like strategic planning. It's more than an intellectual exercise. It helps you control your destiny and reduce stress. When I talk about strategic planning, I'm not talking about things like figuring out how big the total U.S. market is for HVAC projects through the year 2014— that kind of data means little to me. Just about every market served by our industry is big, and it's rare to find a company that has even one-half of one percent of any of them. I'm more interested in philosophy and implementation.

Philosophy for the firm is defined by articulating the mission (why the company exists) and strategies (how will you go about doing business in marketing, accounting, operations, human resources, ownership transition, etc.) for the firm. Once the mission and strategies are agreed upon, implementing change is a snap.

Firm owners, like home owners, get into trouble when:

1. **They don't define what the firm is all about.** For example, "Do we want a full-service A/E firm or a high-design architectural firm?" This is analogous to, "Do we want a colonial-style or a contemporary-style house?" Leaving these questions unresolved creates the potential for arguments over every single minor decision that follows— whether it's about purchasing, the kind of training to invest in, or keeping an unprofitable branch office open.

2. **They don't plan for the growth.** Everyone wants to grow, but little attention is paid to how to do it. Why open an office in Smallsville, Kansas? Is that really the kind of growth the company wants? Why buy that cheap database program when everything you put into it will be worthless in two years? It's similar to the home owner who turns the garage into a den in the spring and doesn't have anywhere to put his cars when winter arrives. Not planning for growth could lead to arguments over issues

like the amount of capital that should be retained versus the amount that should be paid out in stockholder bonuses. Or how much space should be leased. Or whether to invest in a new computer system.

3. **They don't think about the firm in its totality.** Whether it's home planning or business planning, I always try to consider how changes in one area will affect other areas. For example, a new marketing program might require a lot more personal selling from technical people. Getting that additional effort may require a new incentive compensation plan. This, in turn, might require different accounting to figure out who is doing what. And capturing the sales information might require a new project initiation procedure that is enforced through operations. They are all linked.

4. **They haven't considered a future move.** Just like houses, firms or an individual's interest in a firm will be sold some day. Planning takes that into consideration. The fact is, some firms are worth a lot more than others— they're the ones with strong balance sheets, good internal management, offices in the right locations, and niche positions in hot markets. Proper planning leaves an asset that is desirable, whether the stock is sold to internal buyers or to an outsider. **Z**

D E T A I L S

· ·

FULL-SERVICE, INCLUDING REAL ESTATE: Peter E. Cipriano, P.E., says the key to running a successful realty company along with a consulting engineering firm is to do it all-out or don't do it at all.

"I can name many companies— architects, engineers and constructors— who've dabbled in real estate," says Cipriano, president of El Associates (East Orange, NJ), a 270-person consulting engineering firm, and its sister company, El Realty. "When they dabbled, they got hurt. They generally don't spend the time they should, they're not trained in real estate and they don't specialize. We were in the river so we decided to swim."

El Associates entered the realty arena in 1962. Cipriano says that company is completely separate from the engineering firm; he is the only common link. "It runs its own profit center," says Cipriano. "It has a different management group and different table of organization."

"I think the reason our real estate group took off was because we decided to identify two different companies," says Cipriano. "If we had kept them integrated, clients wouldn't know who they were talking to."

Cipriano says the realty side of El Associates almost always uses its sister company when it needs design work. But occasionally, when the engineering company is too busy, it will go outside for services.

■

WHY BE AN EXPERT WITNESS? For Bill Hime, a principal at Wiss, Janney, Elstner Associates, Inc. (Northbrook, IL), the answer is clear— that's one reason his firm exists. But what about firms whose business is mainly design or consulting? Losing a key principal's hours to an extended court case, especially when that principal normally develops a lot of business, can actually *detract* from a firm's health, says Lee Beetschen, principal at CABE Associates, Inc. (Dover, DE), a 20-person consulting engineering firm.

Beetschen says he charges an inflated rate for expert witness testimony— a minimum of $150 to $200 an hour— for exactly that reason. The time he spends working as an expert witness could be better spent building client relationships or developing new business, he says. "It doesn't bring anything into the firm, other than the money I bring in," says Beetschen. "We have a lot of mouths to feed."

But Carl Schubert, president of 35-person consulting engineering firm Cole/Yee/Schubert & Associates (Sacramento, CA), says he gets personal satisfaction out of contributing to the justice system. He says it also gives him "great insight into the type of mistakes that are being made out there." Others say the exposure is good publicity for the firm.

■

It really works

N OUR business, just like yours, clients are usually happy when you *first* finish a job. But its real value is how well it works *over time.*

Fortunately, we have a number of long-standing client relationships. Based on our experience, here's a short list of management ideas we *know* are working in a wide variety of firms throughout the A/E/P and environmental industry:

1. **Widespread sharing of financial information with all staff.** This is one of the most important keys to building a successful firm without management having to constantly exert its influence over what's happening. Sharing summary financial data on utilization, multiplier, sales, revenues, profits and backlog with all staff gets them doing what they need to *before* a problem gets out of hand. It also provides employees with badly needed feedback that shows they are doing something right when the numbers look good. Not providing this information to your staff is like asking them to fly an airplane without knowing their airspeed, fuel level, altitude, or whether or not their landing gear is down!

2. **Formularized incentive compensation for salaried people.** The bigger a firm gets, the more important this is. One important point— I don't believe that people who are

paid by the hour should get big bonuses. They aren't taking any risk with their extra hours like a salaried person is when they work overtime. But the salaried people should know what they need to do to get their bonus. It shouldn't be a mystery. We have clients who are publishing accrued bonuses monthly, then paying them out quarterly. And they're getting fantastic productivity gains.

3. **Open office environments.** Private offices hurt communications. Ditto for partitions that are too high (more than four or five feet). With an open office, there's much more awareness among team members about what's going on with their projects or with their clients than there is when everyone is locked away. People also learn faster in an open office environment.

4. **Paid business developers— by and large— do not succeed in our business.** And most technical people won't make cold calls. The future of marketing for A/E and environmental firms lies in having a strong marketing support group. Direct mail, original research projects, informative communications that help position the firm as experts in a market sector, getting free press— all of these things are best done by people who have the know-how to do them. Not engineers, architects or scientists who rose to their own level of incompetence and who make two or three times as much as someone better qualified who has the training and experience to succeed in the role.

5. **PC networks and databases.** Just about anything progressive that you want to do today requires a network and a database. Whether it's online time card entry, continuous project management reporting, E-Mail, moving work between work groups, sharing standard specifications and reports, centralizing electronic project filing, or widespread sharing of information on clients, you've got to have a network and a database.

6. **Opportunistic acquisitions.** Because the marketplace is as inefficient as it is, there are tremendous opportunities for buyers and sellers. Payback periods on acquisitions of less than one year are possible with the right deal. For buyers, the key is knowing what you're buying, and paying the right price. For sellers, it's finding the right buyer— one who sees synergies from combining your operation with his.

7. **Team organization structures.** Standing teams or studios, small work groups, and single person reporting all lead to more accountability, fewer meetings, better communications, improved quality, better service, higher utilization, and higher profits. This was all reinforced for me when we did a *second* management audit of a firm we helped reorganize from a matrix to the team concept several years ago. Not only has the firm doubled its staff and increased its revenues almost threefold since then, but everyone knows who they are working for, there are fewer conflicts over workload scheduling, and people are happier.

8. **Ownership incentive compensation tied to percentage of stock held.** Forget internal ownership transition if you don't deal with this one. Any firm that ties all owners into the same perks, privileges, and bonus opportunities, regardless of the percentage of stock they own, is on a crash course. As the firm's value climbs, and older owners with major blocks of stock get out, they will be replaced by five or six or ten other owners with all their associated overhead. That kills profitability. The stock has to be such a good investment that buyers will be willing to make sacrifices to get more. That increases their commitment level. The only way that happens is if profits are paid out in some fashion as a disguised dividend through the incentive system. **Z**

D E T A I L S
• • • • • • • • • • • • • • • • • •

CLIENT CONTACT SOFTWARE TIPS: Client contact software has helped some firms improve their marketing efforts. Here is some advice for firms using (or considering) client contact software.

■ Decentralize. A client contact system can only be really effective if everyone who uses it keeps it updated. That means allowing people "in the field" access to it. They should be able to make changes themselves, not have to send a note to someone at headquarters. Inevitably, a lot of those notes just won't get there.

■ Have one list. Some software products call for each user to maintain a separate database. But some allow information to be communicated to one central location. So users can keep an individual database, but information should be combined in a central location periodically. That helps eliminate duplication of effort and errors.

■ Develop a consistent coding standard. Everyone should use a standard coding system to allow for easier collection of data in a central location. If someone is using his or her own oddball system, much of that person's data could be useless.

■ Code to an internal contact person. When possible, entries should list the name of the closest internal contact person. That helps promote instant recognition, and makes it easier to organize groupings when developing holiday card mailings, invitations, calling lists, and so on.

■ Have a central administrator. One person should be responsible for developing the coding system, reviewing combined information for duplications and errors, and tracking adherence by users.

■ Stress the importance of keeping information up to date. Some people are resistant to computer record-keeping, and others may not see the need to keep information accurate and current. Top management's job is to sell the benefits of an up-to-date, accurate database, and make it a priority for everyone using it.

■

PHONE SMARTS: The receptionist isn't the only person in your firm who directs telephone calls.

Unfortunately, in most firms, "Hold on, I'll *try to* transfer you" is almost guaranteed to be followed by a dial tone. We were cut off three times in a row recently at one firm. The culprit was the *marketing director*!

Imagine how much business is lost through "transferred" phone calls that never reach their destination. Make sure everyone in the firm knows how to use the phone system.

■

Join the computer age

LOTS OF FIRMS in the A/E and environmental consulting business point with pride to their commitment to technology. They talk about their "state-of-the-art" CADD systems, custom-designed programs for structural analysis, and GIS capabilities, and make free use of all the latest high-tech jargon.

While it's understandable that firms are proud of what they can do (a good self-image is a prerequisite for a successful firm), many should take a little closer look at themselves before bragging too loudly. I have never claimed to be a computer expert, but much of what I have seen lately reinforces what my old friend Mike Latas has been saying for years— "Common sense is not so common":

1. **Computers are still not networked.** This goes for both technical computers and business computers (many times they are one in the same). What this means is that people cannot easily share files, or printers, nor can they communicate electronically. Also important— there is no good way to do a regular back-up. Think about disaster planning.

2. **Big firms still don't have electrostatic plotters.** To me, a design firm of any significant size (30-40 people or more) that doesn't have an electrostatic plotter is like a

newspaper without a photocopier, or a mechanic without an engine analyzer.

3. **Even big firms won't hire a high-powered person for computing functions.** Staying on top of this whole business of computerization requires intelligent people. We've pretty much figured that out in the marketing, finance, and human resources areas for our industry. Now we need to apply the same thinking to our computing function. And don't forget, smart people cost money.

4. **Firms are not using macros.** This really kills me, because macros— recording and playing back the keystrokes to perform a particular task— are not that hard to set up. Why don't firms have macros for letters, meeting minutes, and memos? That makes all of the products look consistent, in addition to saving oodles of time.

5. **Firms haven't figured out what their electronic filing conventions will be.** You will never get the most out of CADD or even out of your word processing system if you don't have standard ways of filing things and standard file naming schemes. That's how you can find this stuff later and re-use it— and not least important, know that you're using the most current version of the file.

6. **Firms still have not placed a computer on everyone's desk.** Stop making excuses. Get past your aversion to leasing and get the equipment your people need now. You wouldn't send soldiers out in the field to do battle and then tell them to share a single rifle would you? We *are* in a battle— a competitive battle.

7. **Firms are not buying enough notebook/laptop computers.** Make it easier for people to take work home. And notebooks *are* something that more than one person can share.

8. **Firms are not offering enough training.** If you are going to get the most out of your computers, you will have to spend money on training. Once again, refer to the soldier example above— no responsible commander would send his or her "soldiers" into the battlefield without adequate training.

9. **Firms are not setting company-wide computing standards for what goes on what CADD layer.** This just means that it's harder to coordinate disciplines, harder to move work between offices, harder to change staff on a project in mid-stream, harder to make changes, and harder to figure out what you did before. The same is true when firms are not using the same software in all locations for word processing, spreadsheets, databases, and so on.

10. **Firms don't have good databases.** Become a learning organization and start to capturing all you do— who you are selling to, what you are doing for those companies, and who your staff is calling on to get new work. Then in five years, give me a call and tell me whether or not you are better off than your competition.

11. **Firms are trying to run Windows with inadequate hardware.** Everyone is going to Windows, the main benefit of which in my mind is not ease of use but the ability to do multi-tasking (have more than one software application running at the same time). Yet they are trying to run it on computers with no RAM. Get 8 megs for every machine at a minimum! Otherwise, stick to DOS, which still works fine for many.

12. **There's no master spec available to the engineers and architects.** Instead, the spec from a similar job is recalled and edited to fit the current job. Then people wonder why the firm looks stupid when the wrong job name is used, the current codes aren't complied with, and products that haven't been available for years are specified.

With the incredible decline in computer prices over the last few years, I refuse to believe that any firm can't afford to stay up to date, if it really wants to. The *real* reason we aren't keeping up is that the typical design firm principal is over 50, was not trained on a PC, and doesn't use one every day. As a result, he or she really doesn't understand the power of computing and what it can do for the business in terms of providing a strategic advantage over its competitors. **Z**

D   E   T   A   I   L   S

"THE PACE with which computer technology is moving forward seems to be gaining momentum every month... Of particular importance is understanding what new 3D modeling capabilities can do for you and what they cannot...

"Not too many years ago, using advanced modeling and visualization tools required expensive computer hardware and software systems... That has changed dramatically in the past few years. Programs such as AutoCAD and MicroStation include 3D modeling and visualization software as part of the basic package...

"A recent survey asked why visualization was not being used more extensively. The consistent response was that the programs were too hard to use. Where firms were using the technology effectively, it was frequently due to a staff member spending personal time to become proficient. It was only then that these firms realized the value of using visualization and animation software as both marketing and project design tools."

SOURCE: David E. Weisberg in *A/E/C Computer Solutions*, January-February 1994.

MORE ON COMPUTERS: Any firm of more than 20 or 30 people that refuses to appoint a qualified MIS manager or PC coordinator because of an aversion to hiring any more "support" people, is being penny-wise and pound foolish.

What happens in these companies? Here is a typical scenario: Systems planning and design falls to "Anne," the architect who has a "knack" for setting up homespun, convoluted solutions because she's never seen a system set up the right way.

Troubleshooting is done by "Bill," the CADD technician who's the only person around who knows how to copy a file to a floppy disk.

Finally, "Tony," the mechanically inclined engineering co-op student (he changes his own oil), is the one staffer who knows how to remove the case screws on a PC and install an expansion board— but he's not here this semester.

While these dabblers try to hold the system together with the computing equivalent of rubber bands and chewing gum, everyone else waits till they can get back to work on the firm's real business. And in the end, the "remedies" they implement are more painful and costly to fix than the original problems.

Keep your expectations realistic

EVERY FIRM in this industry must do four things to survive— *sell* work, *do* work, *bill* for work, and get *paid* for work. That's it. If you ask me, architects, engineers, and environmental consultants (along with their advisors) do a *wonderful* job of making what should be a simple business too complicated. Consider the following:

- **How can you expect to sell work if you haven't even identified who can buy your services?** 98% of A/E/P and environmental firms have never taken the time to identify all the organizations that could possibly buy their services, much less everyone in those organizations who can make or influence the purchase decision. This is where marketing starts— by identifying buyers. With this kind of haphazard marketing process, is it any wonder so many firms struggle to get work? You need a company-wide client database to get a handle on the problem.

- **How can you expect to sell work if your sales people don't even know your capabilities?** Every day, we see firms with such disorganized marketing information that the people doing the selling can't even find out what their company has previously done for a specific client. We also see situations where people doing the selling are completely unaware that one of the firm's employees used to work for the client. Most firms have no method to ensure that this never happens. Once again, you need a company-wide marketing database.

■ **How can you expect to do good work if you have no control over the people who are supposed to turn it out for you?** The most common form of organization structure for an A/E/P or environmental firm is a matrix based on a combination of project managers and production units. And it doesn't work. The matrix virtually prohibits accountability. It ensures that those doing the selling have no power to deliver on their promises. Team or studio organization structures work best for most firms in this business.

■ **How can you expect to do good work if you never find out what your clients think about it?** Only 25% of firms always ask for a client debriefing after failing to get a job. An even smaller percentage actually take the time to poll their clients regularly to find out just how happy they are with the services the firm has provided. This is the perfect role for the PIC, who otherwise might be sitting on his or her rear. It also justifies hiring an objective third party to poll your clients every couple of years.

■ **How can you expect to bill for work if you don't have complete and up-to-date information on the time spent on the job by each individual working on it?** Collecting time sheets once or twice a month is not enough, especially for firms doing lots of small jobs (the bulk of the industry). The budget is busted before the P.M. has seen the first report. Most firms desperately need on-line project time recording and management reporting.

■ **How can you expect to bill for work if you don't have all the suppliers' bills related to the job?** Most firms in this business take days or even weeks to input and schedule invoices received for payment. Why should it take so long? Get caught up, then input every invoice to your system the day you get it. You should only go through the process of getting approval from the appropriate project manager (or principal) *after* the invoices are entered into your accounts payable system.

■ **How can you expect to get paid for work if your bill doesn't get to the client?** Most firms take between four and 20 days to get bills out after all of the time sheets are collected. Why so long? Everything should be ready to go so when the time spigot is shut off, or the regular billing cycle comes around, the bill can immediately go out the door.

■ **How can you expect to get paid for work if your bill doesn't make sense?** Pull out 10 of your most recent invoices. Do you understand everything on them? If *you* don't, how in the world is your client going to? Why do so many firms send out bills that are called "statements," or bills that have all kinds of unintelligible garbage written all over them like internal project reference codes, obscure task/phase/activity references, and so on? If you do it because your accounting system puts them out that way, change it. Or port the data to the word processor and fix it there.

Selling, doing, billing, and *getting paid* for work— that's what it's all about. But don't expect to do any better in these areas if you aren't willing to change. **z**

Lean on me

WATCHED a movie on T.V. the other night titled "Lean on Me," starring one of my favorite contemporary actors, Morgan Freeman. Freeman played Joe Clark, an inner-city high school principal who had one year to get two-thirds of his student body to pass a "Minimum Basic Skills" test. Although he started with a mess, in the end, he prevailed. It was a classic turnaround situation, and many of Clark's tactics could be useful to principals and managers working in troubled A/E/P and environmental consulting firms.

1. **Turnarounds require a single, strong leader.** The first thing Clark did was get all of his teachers together and let them know that he, and only he, was in charge. He did not create a committee to study the school's performance problems, but instead enacted a state of "martial law." Although there certainly are exceptions, most A/E and environmental firms with multiple owners— none of whom controls a majority of stock— could benefit from being less democratic. We waste too much time getting everyone's support before doing anything. And all too often, the support is superficial, and the passive-aggressive resistors get their way in the end, anyway.

2. **Turnarounds require a good house cleaning.** One of the first things Joe Clark did was throw out the kids that

were lazy or caused trouble. That made it easier for the remaining students to succeed. He realized that the no-good students were dragging down the good students. He was more concerned about the welfare of the school and the good students than he was the bad ones. We need more of that thinking in this business! Just about every firm I go into has people on the payroll who haven't carried their weight for years. It's sad that top management lets these people drag down the rest of the firm because no one wants to be "mean." And we're not doing the non-performers any favor, either. Every day that goes by makes it harder for them to start over somewhere else, doing something they like better or find more rewarding.

3. **Turnarounds require that management accepts blame for the current state of affairs.** Joe Clark called all of his teachers together and told them that they were failing, that they were responsible for the kids' poor performance. He didn't blame the terrible home situations, the crime problem, or drugs. Sure, he acknowledged that it was a hostile environment, but that didn't change his feeling that the school and the teachers were responsible. The same goes for an A/E or environmental consulting firm. When things get bad, rarely is the staff the problem, though I've heard more than one principal in my day cry that. The problem is management, and I'm talking about top management. Like anyone who has a problem, the first step to recovery is to accept responsibility for it. When things go sour we need to take a closer look at ourselves, rather than look for someone else to blame.

4. **Turnarounds require a heavy dose of discipline.** Clark was a fanatic about order. He repainted the entire school and got the students on detention to help out with the cleaning. He also demanded every student learn the school song. He knew the students would be better equipped for life if he forced some discipline on them. He also knew the teachers would be better off if they felt that they, too, could be successful. As an industry, A/E and

environmental firms have a long way to go with discipline— architectural and environmental consulting firms, in particular. We allow people to work in disorder approaching squalor. Managers get away without doing their staff's performance appraisals. People charge time to marketing and don't turn in a client contact report. Job numbers are issued without having a contract. All of this happens because we have no discipline. We are afraid to insist on anything for fear someone will get upset. But my reaction to that is: "Why are you so worried about getting those people upset? They obviously don't care if they upset you (by not complying)."

5. **Turnarounds require a good team.** While a strong leader is required, the rest of the team is important, too. Everyone has to do their part to make the organization a success. To get the most out of everyone, you can't scream at them all of the time— you can't use just "the stick." You need "the carrot," too. Clark forgot that until his assistant principal set him straight. Most engineers, architects, and scientists could benefit from a little sensitivity training. Everyone appreciates a "please," a "thanks," and a little recognition for putting in the extra effort. Money always says "thank you" in a meaningful way, but that requires that the firm be a success. First comes the performance, then the rewards.

6. **Turnarounds require a leader who can take the heat.** As I'm sure you can imagine, some of what Clark did wasn't popular in the school and with the community. Lots of people were out to get him. But he didn't care. His allegiance was to the students and to his boss. Fortunately for Clark, he had some friends in high places who were able to defend him just long enough that he could be successful. The same applies to our business. Turnarounds seem to be the most successful when initiated by an inside CEO— usually someone who is new to the job but not to the company— with some outside help and intervention from a good consultant or outside board member.

Outside CEOs (i.e., those hired from outside the firm) often fail because they don't have the strong political base required to buy the time that they need to emerge victorious in the end. **Z**

Lessons from the new Chrysler Corporation

NYONE WHO KNOWS me will tell you I'm a "car" guy. I've always been nuts about them— I knew every car on the road by the time I was three. That's why in addition to following what's going on in the A/E/P and environmental consulting industries, I read *everything* I can about automobiles and their makers.

The rejuvenation of Chrysler Corporation, especially when contrasted with what's happening at Chrysler's biggest domestic competitor— General Motors— can be a real inspiration for those of us working in the professional service industries. In 1993, Chrysler Corporation was more profitable than Ford and G.M. combined— as well as more profitable than *all* of the Japanese auto makers combined. Who would have thought that would ever be possible?

To discover why they are so successful, let's look at what Chrysler has been doing:

■ **Chrysler is developing new products in record time.** While I'm generally conservative and believe in "sticking to one's knitting," I also believe in the need to constantly come out with something new. Even if it's a new and better packaging of something that already exists, or a refinement of an existing product or service offering, this constant push for something *new* keeps an organization vital. Whether this "new" product is a packaged audit service to help a hospital client optimize the use of their space, forensic engineering services, lead paint consulting, or lighting design, you've got to have something new to sell on a regular basis. Think about your own firm— what do you have to offer your clients that's *new*?

■ **Chrysler is re-using what they have done before.** All of the auto-makers are getting better and better about reducing the number of "platforms" and drivetrains for their car lines, but Chrysler is doing this especially well. The reason is simple— it saves money and improves quality. The same thing applies to A/E and environmental consulting firms. One of the greatest efficiency gains for any firm in *this* business lies in really getting organized in information storage and retrieval. Most of us are really in the *publishing* business— we put out plans, specifications, and written reports. We have to be able to find the stuff we've already done and be able to re-use it when it makes sense to do so. That takes *planning, organization,* and *implementation!*

■ **Chrysler has a radical organization structure.** Instead of doing it like G.M., where everything is departmentalized (as it is in the typical design or environmental firm's discipline departments), Chrysler puts the marketing people, the design people, the financial people, and the manufacturing people working on a car line all in *one* organizational unit. The old barriers and territorial boundaries are down. Communication goes up. Quality improves. Decision making is faster. This is precisely the kind of thinking we need more of in our business.

■ **Chrysler is investing heavily in R&D.** A few years ago, when Chrysler spent a bundle to build their massive research and development center where new technologies are tested and new cars are created, everyone thought they were crazy. The Wall Street experts openly predicted their demise. But Chrysler had a bigger idea in mind, beyond just optimizing short-term profits. Because they bit the bullet and made some short-term sacrifices, Chrysler is now in a position where they can create a new car faster than any of their competitors. Think about what you are doing to invest in R&D. Most firms in *this* business are doing virtually *nothing!*

■ **Chrysler's top executives aren't sitting around figuring out how to spend all their loot on new perks for themselves.** When Chrysler's new chairman inherited the executive suite from his predecessor, he didn't change one stick of furniture or stitch of decor— he kept it exactly as it was. Contrast this with G.M.'s 14th floor. While a graduate student advisor to a group of business school students who won an intercollegiate marketing competition sponsored by G.M. in 1979, I got to spend a few days with their top executives in Detroit. To say they live like royalty in the executive suite is an understatement— it's *lavish.* They even had two people waiting on each one of us in the executive dining room at lunch! Think about your own firm— are the top managers treated like royalty? If so, watch out for the serfs. They'll eventually rise up and storm the castle walls!

■ **Chrysler is competing on more than just price.** Look at the ads they're running on national T.V. or in the magazines. How many mention the price of the car? Now take a look at G.M.'s advertising. From top to bottom, with *very* few exceptions, the *price* of the vehicle is what they are promoting. Why do you think that is? Because G.M. can't sell anything else. They don't have the quality, the design, or the features the market wants. That's precisely the same trap too many professional services firms fall into. They won't abandon the cheap market and end up reducing quality to the lowest possible level. They, too, end up competing only on price. Whether it's cars or subdivision design, being the cheapest is rarely ever the way to be the most successful over time.

Let's all do what we can to model our firms after the *winners*, not the *losers*. The entire A/E/P and environmental consulting industry could benefit. **z**

Making direct mail work

A SOLID majority of firms who use direct mail in their marketing efforts are less than thrilled with the results. In fact, according to our newly published *1994 Marketing Survey of A/E/P and Environmental Consulting Firms*, 13% consider this the *least* successful marketing strategy they have employed and only 5% consider it part of their most successful strategy. While I believe that was the experience of those who responded to our survey, I know from my own experience that direct mail *can* work if it's implemented properly. Here's where we see firms go wrong:

1. **The firm doesn't have a large enough prospect list.** This is the most common problem for A/E or environmental consulting firms using direct mail. Many firms think someone should not be added to the list unless he or she has done business with the firm or is known personally by a principal or other key staff member. But the list is not the place to pre-screen opportunities— it should include virtually everyone who could buy or influence the decision to buy your firm's services.

2. **The firm is not mailing frequently enough.** Direct mailers in other industries often call it "Chinese water torture" when they mail to the same list over and over until the respondent finally breaks down and buys something.

That may mean mailing to the same group 12, 18, or even 24 times in a year, not just two or three times.

Some people think that's too expensive. Yet most mailings can be accomplished for under 30 cents per piece, if bulk mail is used and the cost of printing is controlled. Or they say it takes too long to design a mailing with all the necessary approvals. That's often because every principal wants to put *his or her* stamp of approval on it, bogging down the process.

3. **The firm has unrealistic expectations for a response rate.** I often hear numbers like 5% or 10% bandied about as targeted response rates, but believe me, if those numbers were possible to get consistently, we could all retire tomorrow! A 1%, or even .5% response rate is the norm— but that's not bad. If you have enough numbers on the list (2,000 or 20,000 instead of 200 in a specific market *sector*), and you mail often enough, a 1% response rate on 2,000 pieces of mail to one group of clients would produce 20 inquiries. And it might cost you as little as $600! One technical person with a $75-per-hour billing rate could *easily* chew that up on one sales call.

4. **The firm doesn't track its results.** You need the numbers to know what's going on. When you *know* the kind of results you are getting, you can control the risk. I haven't figured out how firms know what works and what doesn't— I've only seen a handful in my entire career that actually *track* inquiries from new clients and their source.

5. **The firm aims its direct mail at *all* clients instead of just one group.** "Shot-gunning" is another *big* problem with the direct mail of A/E/P and environmental consulting firms. It seems just about everyone does it— even the largest firms. We're seeing more companies sending out super-expensive, flossy and glossy, four-color magazines, covering everything from work in Siberia to new offices acquired in Nevada to park preservation projects in South Georgia. There is no way all of that could interest any

one particular client. The result is a lot of expense and little reaction.

6. **The firm doesn't get a response because it doesn't ask for one.** You should always ask for a response *or* give away some information that the respondent will value (see point #7). Failing to ask for a response is like sending out a catalog and not providing an order form or 800 number. The *point* of all this mail is to persuade clients to call and *buy* the services the firm provides (or at least give the firm a chance to investigate the need and see if they can help).

7. **The firm uses direct mail to brag instead of to provide information valued by clients.** Most of the direct mail we see boasts about past projects, new capabilities or who was promoted to "senior associate." Direct mail should instead inform clients of important regulatory changes, share research results from unique studies they've completed, or offer other truly helpful information the client will keep close by for easy reference. The bragging stuff just goes in the trash can.

Before *your* firm closes the door on direct mail, consider that the problem may lie in how you *implement* it, not with the concept as a whole. *Good* direct mail *should* be a part of your firm's complete marketing program. **Z**

D E T A I L S

. . . .

DIRECT mail can be an extremely effective means of marketing. Unfortunately, many A/E/P and environmental consulting firm principals blow the whole marketing budget on developing a slick, four-color brochure jammed with cliches and buzzwords, then send it off to every name on the company rolodex. Not only are about a quarter of the brochures returned because the company has moved or the recipient has left the firm (or died), but the brochure generates absolutely no new business.

A direct mail campaign, if it is well conceived, planned, and followed up on, does not have to cost a fortune, require an inordinate amount of time, or end up as the company joke.

Following are some suggestions for designing and implementing an effective direct mail campaign:

Tailor your program to meet a specific need. "Define what drives your industry and then gear your marketing program around it," recommends Marshall Miller & Associates, Inc.'s officer/operations manager, Ellen Allen.

Allen, knowing that environmental regulation compliance deadlines were imminent, contacted the owners of underground storage tanks near the company's Bluefield, VA, headquarters office. She sent letters to them asking if they knew what they had to do to comply with the new regulations. That ten hour time investment generated at least 100 *qualified* leads and ended in 20 or more *real* jobs for the environmental consulting firm.

"You have to fill a need. We sat down and said, 'Let's design something that people want to read about— no one wants to read a company brochure,'" says Mary Burton, marketing director of the 80-employee, Blacksburg, Virginia, consulting engineering firm Draper Aden Associates, Inc. Accordingly, Burton began work on the firm's first tipping fees report in 1989 when she realized that many localities in the state were ignorant of their neighbors' landfill tipping fees.

Burton created a simple questionnaire and sent it to a specific list of potential clients. She developed a report based on the responses and mailed it back to the participants. That original report generated a slew of telephone calls. Years later Draper Aden still publishes the report and is widely recognized as a leading expert in landfill and water and sewer design.

Develop a targeted mailing list. Half the battle in a direct mail campaign is knowing who to send material *to*. Says Allen, "I'm very averse to mass mailings where you send out a thousand letters and hope that a few stick. I like to practice what I call 'Lean and mean guerrilla marketing'— target in and know who you're sending to."

Follow up. Once the report is complete, send copies of it with press releases to the trade journals. Publications that *clients* read and where clients and the survey participants are located should not be overlooked, says Burton.

■

Now's the time to buy (or sell)

NO MATTER WHAT the self-appointed experts are telling you, right now is a *great* time to buy a firm or to be acquired by or merge with another firm. But, like most things, it's not going to last forever. From our perspective, the merger, acquisition, and divestiture business within the A/E and environmental consulting industry is at an all-time peak. There seems to be more activity every day. Let's review what's fueling this frenzy:

1. **Interest rates are at an historical low.** This means that it's cheap and easy for good firms to borrow money. In fact, banks are *looking* for firms that are in a good financial position to lend money to. Many of our financially strong clients tell us that their bankers are reacting enthusiastically to smart acquisition proposals. Being able to get the money is critical— cash is the lubricant that makes acquisition deals happen.

2. **You can't get a better return from other, "safer" investments.** Rates of return on bank accounts and money markets don't look very appealing and there aren't lots of other alternatives available to investors who want a high return at a fairly low risk. No wonder firm acquisitions look attractive in this climate. However, rest assured, if

interest rates ever go back up to 14% or 18%, you won't see much interest in buying and selling A/E or environmental consulting firms.

3. **There are lots of buyers and sellers in the marketplace.** No market would exist without both buyers and sellers, and hardly a day goes by that our phones don't ring with someone who either wants to buy or sell. In fact, 22% of those who responded to our 1994 *Principal's Survey of A/E/P & Environmental Consulting Firms* indicated that their firm had acquired, been acquired by, or merged with another entity. And, no doubt an even greater number have attempted to do something, yet failed for one reason or another.

4. **Experienced buyers abound.** Once firms figure out that they can buy another company and make it work, both culturally and economically, they tend to do it again and again. One of our clients has successfully purchased 14 companies since 1989. Another has acquired seven firms or unwanted satellite offices of other companies. These veteran buyers know how to talk to sellers, are reasonable in their offers, come armed with alternative deal structures, and are knowledgeable about how to make things work once a merger, sale, or acquisition is consummated.

5. **Satellite offices and captive firms are being spun off.** There was a time when firms pursued geographical expansion just for the sake of being able to claim they had so many offices in the state or the country. That is *over*. Smart companies figured out that they need a *good* reason to establish another satellite office, because office proliferation complicates everything. Ditto for companies whose primary business is not in the design or environmental consulting industries— many are starting to question the wisdom of trying to do everything in-house, and some are disposing of in-house groups and outsourcing these services.

6. **It *can* work out.** No one should deny that there are lots of
ways to go *wrong* when buying or selling a firm, yet it
doesn't have to be the proverbial "mine field" that all of
the one-man consultants will tell you it is. There are a
number of companies out there today, firms already
working in our industry, whose owners will get rich because of their aggressive acquisition campaigns. These
firms are headed by driven, entrepreneurial leaders who
are both good deal-makers and good managers. They
know how to make things work. And they long ago got
past the idea that it is necessary to do or touch everything in the business themselves, an idea that so many
design professionals get programmed into them early in
their careers. These leaders have learned to delegate and
have a high tolerance for ambiguity.

Every design or environmental consulting firm ought to
have strategies prepared for how they will search out (or at
the very least how they will *react* to) merger, sale, and/or acquisition opportunities. The time has never been better to
capitalize on the opportunities that are all around us. Decide
how you and your firm can cash in now, before these opportunities evaporate. Nothing lasts forever. **Z**

D E T A I L S

▪ ▪

MERGER & ACQUISITION SECRETS: How do buyers find sellers? How do sellers find buyers? How do both parties strike a deal that works?

If you want to buy:

■ Find the firms you like, *then* see if they're interested. Define exactly what you want (size, services, location, etc.). Identify and contact *every* firm that meets those criteria. (See the list of research sources below).

■ If vertical integration is your goal, don't overlook your subconsultants. You've already had a chance to evaluate them.

■ Avoid business brokers. They lack clout with the firms they supposedly represent. And their situation is riddled with conflicts of interest (the fee, or the bulk of it, is contingent on closing the deal).

■ Do, however, be open-minded to opportunities that may surface— sometimes these are the best deals.

If you want to sell or merge:

■ Other design and environmental firms are your best possibilities. Research firms that provide similar services in a different region or complementary services in your region. And contact 100 or more firms, not just five or ten. Look at the directories published by *ENR*, *ACEC*, *NSPE*, *AIA*, and others.

■ Use an intermediary. A trusted intermediary can make first contact with potential buyers without revealing your identity. Then you pursue the attractive ones. Good choices include a management consultant, lawyer, or accountant. However, beware business brokers who work on a contingent fee basis (see above).

■ "Blind box" advertisements announcing "firm for sale" are usually fruitless. However, it doesn't hurt to give it a try, as long as it's not your only tactic.

Buyers and sellers:

■ If you're serious, try to generate multiple possibilities. The fall-off rate is high. Too many firms get stuck negotiating with a single party.

■ Strive for a win-win situation in any deal. When the merger/acquisition doesn't work, it's almost always because one party went in feeling they got "screwed." Then they're looking to get even.

■

Ownership transition dilemma

AS WE'VE pointed out before, a minority owner's shares in a design and environmental consulting firm are usually worth less than the pro rata share of the company's worth if it were to be sold in its entirety. Recently, we were presented with the following illustration of this principle in action.

John Johnson, the majority shareholder of Johnson Architects and Planners (not his real name or firm name) is ready to retire, and associates in the firm have been selected to acquire the stock over a five-year period. Upon completion of the deal all shareholders will own equal amounts of the stock (there will be no majority shareholder). However, during the transition period, John will not only continue to own more than 50% of the stock through the *second* year, he will remain the single biggest stockholder through the *fourth* year of the transition.

On one hand, the buyers of these minority shares are probably entitled to purchase the stock at a discount since they will not be able to control the cash flow, perquisites, or the company's direction until the final year of the transition. On the other hand, John wants to get fair market value for his majority position in his firm.

Following are four alternative ways to work this out:

1. **The associates pay a discount for the minority shares purchased in the first four years.** In the final year, when the buyer gains controlling interest, the shares will probably be worth *at least* their pro rata share of the company's net worth. This is a very common solution for internal ownership transition, where stock is frequently *undervalued*. However, it doesn't really meet John's expectation of full market value.

2. **The associates buy John's stock outright and fund the acquisition with a note co-signed by the firm.** John receives his current fair share of the company with a guaranteed note (over a reasonable time period), and the buyers have immediate control of the cash flow and perquisites they are paying for. If the buyers do not make the payments on the note, the stock automatically defaults to the company's treasury stock. This is another common solution, but in this case John must have real faith in the ability of his associates to run the firm profitably and meet their commitments.

3. **John and the buyers sign side agreements on cash flow, perquisites, and other issues that could affect the anticipated cash flow of the firm.** This may address the concerns of the buyers that John will still be calling all the shots, but can be very cumbersome and may not result in a good relationship between John and the new owners.

4. **All shareholders agree to vote on a simple majority basis, not as a percentage of their stock holdings, for all business issues.** Here, John is giving up a degree of control in exchange for a higher payout.

John's firm is leaning toward solution #4. But, as this case illustrates, there are no easy answers. Since each case is different, consult qualified advisors before implementing any of the options in your firm. **Z**

Pearls of wisdom

I F YOU'VE worked in the A/E, consulting engineering, or environmental consulting business for *any* time, you've heard all the old adages, or "pearls of wisdom." These are the phrases that endure— words spoken throughout the halls of the company, from cubicles to board rooms. Most employees with a lick of sense wouldn't dare challenge these "truths." To do so might be career suicide, as these are the unwritten laws that govern the individual behavior of employees and managers in firms throughout our industry or profession. Let's take a look at a few of these:

"Never say anything bad about the competition." This has always been one of my favorites, and I've been hearing it since I got my first real job at The Kirkwood Cycle Shop when I was twelve. But as I got older, I learned that running down the competition may be necessary. And it *can* be an effective selling tactic if done discreetly. I'd like to see this pearl changed to: "Never say anything bad about the competition— *unless it's true.*" To me, there's an ethical issue in *not* telling your client what you know. After all, if you *really* cared about your clients, you would want them to avoid making a bad decision by hiring the wrong firm, wouldn't you?

"Pay should be based on performance." Intuitively, this makes sense. No one *wants* to pay a lot of money to someone who performs badly. But in reality, you can have the very best performing office clerk in the world, and there is only so much you can pay someone in that role. Yet, you could have the worst hydrogeologist in the world, and if you wanted to get that person on board (so you could find out how bad they *really* were), you would have to pay more for him or her than you would for your superstar clerk.

"The technical people who produce the work are every bit as important as those who sell or manage it." As *people*, in terms of their pure human potential, undoubtedly they *are* as important. But when you add three words to the phrase— important "to the company"— the statement isn't true. For every 20 people in the business who are competent technically, only *one* of them can do the technical work *plus* sell and manage. The law of supply and demand virtually ensures that the seller and manager will *always* be more important to the company than one who only produces. Yet, as managers working in A/E or environmental firms, we don't seem to want to come to grips with this fact, and communicate it to our people.

"You can't share the firm's financial information with the staff because: A) They won't understand it, B) It could end up in the hands of the competition, or C) It'll make them so scared that they'll jump ship." This kind of thinking is really from the "old school," yet pervades management today. My response is: A) Very few stupid people work in this industry— maybe they can figure out more than you think, and if they can't, give them the training they need so they can. B) We are so *un*competitive in this business that it doesn't matter. If something did end up in the hands of the enemy— they wouldn't do anything with it, anyway. C) If you track the *right* information that *predicts* problems before they occur, maybe your people will do something before it gets to be a problem *without* management having to tell them to do it— and save their jobs in the process.

"Debt is bad. You're always better off paying cash for something instead of leasing it." This kind of thinking has gotten more growing firms in trouble than most people would believe. Being overly debt-averse can kill a company. By using up all of the operating capital for capital expenditures instead of to cover uncollected accounts receivable, a growing firm can find itself unable to finance its own cash flow and end up at the mercy of a dispassionate bank or other creditors.

"We don't have enough work so we have to get more proactive with our marketing." This statement *may* be true, but more often, it is not. The typical A/E or environmental consulting firm wastes the bulk of its marketing resources responding to project opportunities that it has little chance of getting, and as a result, does a lousy job responding on jobs it *should* get. What good is it to be more proactive and develop more possibilities that the firm won't close? Maybe the answer to the lack of work problem lies in doing a better job *reacting* to the opportunities that come in the door, instead of creating more of them. ▪

D E T A I L S

BAD ADVICE: There are a lot of management newsletters— and even more management consultants— aimed at the A/E/P and environmental consulting industry. Some of what these so-called "gurus" put out is valuable; some of it is ridiculous. Here are some things that we have seen printed or espoused elsewhere that we think are garbage:

■ *Instead of a CEO, have an executive committee.*

This is a classic cop-out that is often suggested by management consultants who do not have the guts to tell their clients that only one of them can be the CEO. In the long term, we have yet to see a firm successfully replace a CEO with an executive committee.

■ *Eliminate janitorial services and make your staff responsible for cleaning the office at the end of the day. Buy the pizza and the beer, pick a rotating team and you'll still be ahead.*

I cannot imagine any professional in an A/E/P or environmental firm who thinks he or she should have to take out their own garbage or vacuum their own office. Perhaps an exception might be the proprietor of a very small firm. This is "penny-wise and pound-foolish."

■ *Discontinue in-house lunches, or eliminate lunch meetings and replace them with breakfast meetings.*

I guess the thinking here is that lunches are a more expensive meal than breakfast, but a lunch is pretty cheap when you consider you may get an hour's worth of additional productivity (the average billing rate in an A/E/P or environmental firm is probably $50 per hour), or an hour's worth of training that you wouldn't get if you hadn't spent the $3.50.

■ *Use old blueprints to wrap packages instead of brown wrapping paper.*

This suggestion is so ridiculous, it borders on the absurd. You have to be kidding. Can you imagine the impact of a clerk mistakenly sending out something in blue prints for a military project that your firm designed, and having that get back to the client?

■ *Clean office drawers to collect pencils, pens, erasers and paper clips.*

The time spent doing it isn't worth the reward.

■ *Lock the supply cabinet and make everyone turn in their pencil stubs to get a new one.*

This is a sure-fire morale booster.

■ *Buy ball-point pens instead of felt tip pens.*

If someone told me I couldn't have my Sharpies, I'd say: "Adios."

■

Principal compensation

DECIDING how to reward principals is a perennial problem. Spread out the rewards *equally*, and one principal is bound to feel cheated while another principal gets more than he deserves. *Vary* the compensation of principals, and you'll probably hear complaints and in-fighting, and waste a lot of time with internal politicking.

So how do you determine who gets what, and do it in a way everyone agrees is fair? Here are a few thoughts:

1. **Make sure every principal has a *real* job.** A lot of the bickering I hear related to principals' pay starts with a principal who is perceived by one or more of his peers as not carrying his weight. Every principal, just like every employee, should have a "real" job. To me, that means either being the CEO of the company, the CFO, an office manager, a department manager, a business developer, and so on. It doesn't mean being a "free-floater" who essentially does nothing but go to meetings, call meetings, and take old friends to lunch at the club, but who really can't point to any billable work, sales, or particular management accomplishments at the end of the year.

2. **Let the marketplace determine salaries.** Salary should be set by what the marketplace as a whole is willing to pay for someone with a particular background. You

should be close to the market— not significantly less, nor significantly more. Occasionally, I run into firms that pay salaries that are much lower than the market. This gives them a better-than-normal pre-tax, pre-bonus profit and distorts their sense of managerial well-being. I have also been involved with firms that *thought* they weren't making any profits, when in reality they were paying their profits out in excessive salaries.

There are several industry statistical sources on salaries that can help you determine what the "marketplace" standard is for a particular principal. These sources include D. Dietrich & Associates (Phoenixville, PA); the American Society of Civil Engineers (Reston, VA); the American Institute of Architects (Washington, DC); the National Society of Professional Engineers (Alexandria, VA); and Mark Zweig & Associates. These surveys are by no means a panacea, nor should they set absolute *limits* on what somebody can earn. But they can give you an idea of what's normal for a principal in a particular position in a firm of the same size, type, and location as yours. Have the president/CEO/managing partner set the principals' salaries, except his or her own. Have the board of directors/partners/stockholders set the president's/CEO's/managing partner's salary.

3. **Base bonuses on multiple factors and use a formula to determine specific bonuses.** Be sure to include overall firm performance and share of ownership in the equation, but leave some percentage or portion of "the pot" to address the individual's contribution to the process— through the amount of work he or she has sold, profitability of the business unit he or she is in charge of, and so on. And although I didn't always believe this, as far as I'm concerned, the more you can quantify or "formularize" the incentive compensation system, the better off you'll be. That way, everyone knows the rules, and you'll hear fewer complaints. Just make sure you set up the right rules in the first place, because engineers, archi-

tects, and environmental professionals will figure out what they have to do to get rewarded under those rules, and do it. An example of a "bad" rule would be to pay unit managers' bonuses based on the utilization or chargeability of their work group. You'll end up with high chargeability, but lower multipliers. Every activity remotely related to the job will get charged to it, but the resulting overruns will require much of that supposedly chargeable time to be written off.

Paying all principals the same thing just because they are all owners does not work. No two people have exactly the same role, nor make exactly the same contribution to the firm. On the other hand, anyone not carrying his or her weight should be cut loose, even if that person happens to be a principal. With a company culture that relentlessly clears out the deadwood, you can afford to use some of the more "socialistic" reward schemes that dole out the rewards for principals more equally. Unfortunately, too many A/E/P and environmental firms do not have such a culture. **Z**

D E T A I L S
■ ■

RAISE YOUR LIVING STANDARD: Small firm principals assume a lot of risk and make a lot of sacrifices for their companies. For many, the economic payoff doesn't come until they sell their firms (and for some, not even then). Here are four ways principals in small firms can increase their take-home pay (or decrease their personal expenses). Following each example is the response of an expert, which was solicited when a reader wrote in to question the wisdom of our advice.

■ *Allow principals to trade off salary dollars for a company vehicle. This won't increase your pay, but it lets you pay for your vehicle with pre-tax dollars.*

"You're probably going to get more favorable results deducting a business auto at the corporate level, even if you gain a personal use fringe benefit, than deducting for the business portion of a personal vehicle," says Robert Paul, CPA, partner at Stone and Paul, Certified Public Accountants (Framingham, MA).

■ *Have the company accountant prepare principals' tax returns and bill it to the firm. This is not a legitimate business expense, but the practice is widespread, say accountants.*

Our experts confirmed that personal tax preparation not a legitimate business expense. The practice is wide-spread, however.

■ *If your firm is a C-corporation, switch to an S-corporation status to avoid double taxation. But make*

sure this benefit outweighs any other tax implications.

This is good advice, but only in certain situations, our experts say. They stress that you must analyze your situation and weigh the pluses and minuses of this move.

■ *Reduce salaries for S-corporation shareholders to levels below the FICA maximum and pay out the difference in profit distributions outside of the payroll system. This income is taxable and will show up as a sub-S distribution at the end of the year, but you will save both ends (employer and employee) of the FICA tax. While you're at it, don't forget to make quarterly estimated tax payments, and be forewarned that the Clinton administration is eyeing this loophole.*

"It's true in a sense," says David Wexler of Tofias, Fleishman, Shapiro & Co., P.C. (Cambridge, MA). "But the IRS is aware of the game that can go on and salaries are supposed to be set at market value." In other words, the CEO of a 500-person firm shouldn't take a $20,000 salary and a $200,000 profit distribution. But going from $55,000 to $50,000 would save over $500 in FICA (employee and company portions combined).

Like any publication, we can't provide tax or legal counsel, but these are all ideas that small firm principals should ask their accountant or attorney about.

■

Professionalism

ANYONE in the business of planning, architecture, land surveying, consulting engineering, or environmental consulting knows it's tough. It's hard enough just to survive, much less make money. The same goes for *our* business. We provide professional services, just like our clients. And just like our clients, we have to work hard every day to make our numbers and enhance our reputation.

In any professional service business, you must have a quality team— one that acts "professionally." But not everyone agrees on what the term "professionalism" means. To some people, it means going to professional society meetings or writing technical papers. While those kinds of activities may be a part of it, there's much more. Here's my idea of professionalism:

1. **Always doing what you say you are going to do.** Missing deadlines because you did not work hard enough to meet them or did not plan ahead is unprofessional. Rarely is there ever an acceptable excuse, and professionals know that.

2. **Working hard.** Professionals put in the extra effort it takes to do quality work (and lots of it). Yes— that means hours. Hard work is essential to being successful. It's just like getting in shape physically— simply *wishing* for a hard body

won't make it happen— you have to exercise. The same applies to a profession. You won't be a professional if work is just a nice place you go for 40 hours each week.

3. **Never misrepresenting yourself or your company, and not making promises you can't keep.** Professionals should *never* feel the need to lie or oversell. When it comes to keeping a client happy, nothing is worse than an unkept promise or unmet expectations.

4. **Being honest and trustworthy.** Professionals working in A/E and environmental consulting firms don't attempt to sell their clients anything they don't need, nor do they ever violate their clients' trust and confidence. Clients should know that, at all times, it's their best interests the professional has in mind.

5. **Keeping focused.** Every profession exists to fill a need in society. Every company exists to fill a need in some segment of society. Every employee of a company exists to fill a need in the organization. Professionals *fill* the need and don't get sidetracked. They don't create "busywork" for themselves.

6. **Growing personally.** Your clients, as successful people in their own fields, are interested in personal growth. That means they are learning new things and improving themselves. Long-term success in this business requires personal relationships based on mutual growth. Clients get bored by professionals who do not grow along with them.

7. **Enhancing your client's self-image.** Good professionals understand that their goal is to help their clients feel good about themselves, yet some professionals do the opposite. They think the way to make themselves look good is to show a client how much smarter they are.

8. **Enhancing your own self-image.** Doing the right thing is the best way to feel good about yourself. Helping others feel good helps your self-image, too. Telling other people what you like about them every once in a while versus tearing them down is one way to enhance your self-image.

9. **Feeling good about what you do.** Fortunately, architects, engineers, and scientists are *not* parasites. Your role is absolutely essential. You *do* have the power to help your clients. You can impact a lot of people in a positive way. And the truth is, there aren't many businesses (or professions) that can honestly claim that.

10. **Having the self-discipline to do what needs to be done even if you don't feel like it.** That happens one day at a time. The real professional understands that cleaning up the aftermath of *failure* is far more painful than just *doing* what needs to be done each day.

11. **Not B.S.'ing anyone— ever.** Clients aren't stupid. They know when they are getting crap. To me, "crap" is excuses, cover-your-butt communication, using big words to sound smart when a smaller word would do, poorly thought-out work, shoddy work, false praise, or lousy advice.

12. **Always looking for new opportunities to sell.** Professionals know that they can't practice their profession without having the work to do. They don't push their clients into anything they don't need, but they will gladly sell them anything that they know will help them. In a professional service firm, those who sell will get ahead. Nothing happens without the sale, and professionals aren't afraid to sell.

13. **Thinking.** Professionals are constantly asking themselves if what they are about to do is the right thing for their company and for their client. And if it's not the right thing, they'll take responsibility for convincing the client to do it differently.

14. **Not making a lot of mistakes.** These days, it seems like every manager likes to say he or she *encourages* mistakes. Mistakes are okay if they happen once and no one gets hurt. But the same mistake, repeated over and over again by someone who is supposed to be a professional and know better, is just plain dumb. It's unacceptable and inexcusable— in a word, "unprofessional." **Z**

D E T A I L S

· · · · · · · · · · · · · · · · · · · ·

MARK ASKEW, managing partner at Askew Richardson Hargraves & Associates (Memphis, TN), a 16-person consulting engineering firm, responded to the preceding editorial ("Professionalism"). He specifically addressed item 1, "Always doing what you say you are going to do."

"How many times have we been told by a client, 'We need it on a certain date,' and consequently our people have stayed and worked through the night for several days?" writes Askew. "Only to find out the client was gone the day of the deadline and didn't really need it for another week. Nothing in our profession is more frustrating (with the exception of not getting paid) than to have a client who makes absurd and meaningless deadlines.

"I noticed a phenomenon in our work force that occurs when the client constantly slips the deadline for no apparent reason. I call it 'stress fatigue.' It's like bending a piece of metal, and you keep bending and it gets weaker until it finally breaks. This is similar to a project where the deadline keeps moving and it gets to the point where no one cares about the project anymore, and there's no realistic deadline or goals involved in finishing the project."

Askew also offers his own list describing the traits of a professional client: "One of the greatest acts of a professional is to make it a point to call his consultant on three different occasions: 1. If the consultant is not accepted for a proposal, to let the consultant know why he was not chosen. 2. When a job is well done by a consultant. 3. If the deadline changes."

Askew goes on to write about the satisfaction his staff felt when a client called to praise the structural plans they submitted. "It is the client that never calls when you give the extra effort or tells you that the deadline slipped that is truly unprofessional," he writes.

■

QUOTABLE: "What you've got is two kinds of animals trying to be a third kind of animal."

SOURCE: Ginger S. Evans, construction chief for the new Denver International Airport, explaining in the Feb. 14, 1994 issue of ENR why she would not pick a joint venture to run the project if she had it to do over again. A joint venture of Greiner Engineering, Inc. (Irving, TX) and Morrison Knudsen Engineering, Inc. (Boise, ID), is the program manager for DIA.

■

Quality output

JOHN, the president, CEO, and co-founder of a 250-person Midwestern E/A firm, was frustrated. After so many years of success, it seemed to him that all he was doing now was de-fusing irate clients, talking with lawyers, and dealing with insurance companies. The grim reality of the situation was starting to sink in— his firm had a quality problem.

Sure, John's firm had all of the "usual" QA/QC procedures. The firm used CADD whenever it could. They claimed to make periodic checks along the way during the course of every project by the most senior person in each discipline area. All drawings were reviewed and approved by senior professionals. They even *read* specifications before they went out.

John talked about quality at every company-wide meeting. He appointed a director of QA/QC and started a company-wide quality committee made up of representatives from each discipline to figure out what was wrong and fix it.

Yet, in spite of all these efforts, something in the system was breaking down. Short schedules and tight budgets didn't lend themselves to periodic reviews by senior professionals. No one wanted to let the director of QA/QC look at a project because his time was so expensive it killed the budget. The company-wide quality committee always seemed to be meeting, but couldn't get any of its initiatives adopted, even for seemingly simple things like drawing standards or standard details. And on top of it all, every week there seemed to be a new form to fill out!

John was beside himself. So he finally went off with a couple of his smartest staffers for a long weekend retreat at a nearby resort to map out a new strategy for dealing with the problem. Here's what they came up with:

1. **The firm was trying to build in quality after the fact.** Close examination revealed that just about all of the efforts aimed at quality improvement in John's firm were geared to reviews and corrections *after* the job had been done. With the margins in the A/E business, by then, it's too late.

2. **The firm had the wrong organization structure.** John's firm had the typical matrix structure with discipline departments and project managers who operated outside of those departments, drawing on the necessary resources from each department to accomplish their projects. The problem was that "Sally," an electrical engineer, would find herself simultaneously working on a hospital project, an airport terminal, an auto parts warehouse, and an elementary school, and each one had completely different requirements. She, along with all of the others just like her, could not switch gears fast enough.

3. **The firm was not paying attention to its hiring process.** John's firm always prided itself in good fiscal management. Since labor is always the biggest line item in any A/E or environmental consulting firm, they *never* hired in advance of a need, and added staff only as a last resort. As a result, when they did finally go out to try to hire someone, it was almost always a crisis situation. They ran ads and hired the most nearly qualified person who responded at the moment. Therefore, they got the best of the unemployed and soon-to-be unemployed, people who may have had the technical qualifications to fill their roles— but not the well-rounded "consultants" the firm really needed to be successful in this business.

4. **The principals were disconnected from the business.**
Other than John, only a couple of partners were actively
involved with clients— selling work, managing work, or
doing work. The rest had become full-time administrators
over the years, delegating virtually everything that they
didn't want to do and slowly withdrawing from the real
work of the business. Most were now department heads,
dealing with things such as scheduling problems, or administrators worrying about the returns on the 401(k)
plan, or worse, simply going out to lunch at the club and
getting bombed every day. They didn't know what was going on and weren't applying their expertise to the work.
They were not equipped to do quality reviews, and the
staff did not respect their opinions.

5. **The staff had a negative attitude toward the firm's clients.** Blue-collar attitudes had been tolerated for so long
that the whole culture of John's firm was one of hostility
toward clients (who in reality were the lifeline of the organization). As far as the employees were concerned, the
clients never paid the firm well enough, never gave the
firm enough time to do the job, and wouldn't spend the
money required for the firm to do the job right. Then on
top of it, they were slow to pay their bills when the work
was completed.

6. **The firm never *measured* quality and *reported* on it to
the staff.** Beyond a few of the principals, no one in the
firm *really* knew how many claims the company had
against them. *No one* had any idea of how many jobs required re-work after construction started, or how much
these efforts really cost the firm in terms of lost profits.
And, the firm never undertook any formal effort to find
out what their clients really thought about them.

After their two-day meeting, John went back to the company with a renewed sense of purpose. He eliminated pointless forms that did not contribute to the firm's core process.
He disbanded committees that couldn't get out of first gear.

He made sure that the standards that were set were followed. He overhauled the hiring process to make sure the firm built up a database of candidates in advance of the need. He fired the most obsolete principals, and redirected the others to get back to work again. He set up a team-based organization structure that gave the project managers permanently assigned staff. He implemented a new reward system and gave the first-line supervisors control over wage and salary increase budgets. And, he measured a wide variety of quality indicators and reported on them to all staff each month.

The result— John's firm is back on track, and his work days are more fun again. How about yours? **Z**

Random thoughts

Road Warriors Square Off— My work as a management consultant often takes me out of the state. In fact, not long ago I had to get up at 3:45 a.m. to catch a 6:00 flight from Boston's Logan Airport, the start of a long week to come. After checking my bag, I got on the fully loaded plane around 5:30. At 6:00, they told us our flight was canceled and took us all off the plane because it had a cracked windshield.

As we all waited in a long line to be re-ticketed, one fellow decided to short-cut the process. He went up to the side of the ticket counter and interrupted the airline rep, who dropped what she was doing and spent the next five minutes looking for this guy's ticket, while the rest of us waited our turn.

Of course, everyone in line was furious. Not being in the best of moods myself (I hadn't even had my morning coffee yet), I decided to shout over to the fellow that we were all in a hurry and all had to make other arrangements, and that we'd appreciate it if he waited his turn. (It was a good thing this guy had to go through airport security— at least he didn't have a gun!)

At first, shocked that I said something, the guy asked if I was talking to him. I told him that I was. "You do it your way and I'll do it mine," he said. I told him that the problem was

his way wasn't the right way, that he should be waiting in
line like the rest of us. The crowd cheered me on. He eventually huffed off, and my blood pressure normalized. I thought
to myself, "At least it will be a while before the guy tries that
again."

The point of my story is that some people will *always* try
to work around the system. Whether that means a passenger
butting into line at the airport, or a project manager neglect-
ing to fill out a project initiation sheet and establish the
budget on a new job, the result is the same— other people are
inconvenienced because of one person's lack of consideration.

The real crime is when things like this happen and no one
says anything. If you see someone turning in a late time
sheet, cheating on an expense report, keeping six people waiting a half hour for a meeting to start, or violating the system
in some other way, speak up. Because if you don't, it's possible that no one else will. And if you want your staff to do the
right thing, all of the leaders have to.

Building Management Acceptance of Computers—
Those of us who did not use personal computers in college
are less likely to use one today than our more junior counterparts who grew up on the things. Like many people of my generation in business today, I got into computers out of
necessity. When we started our company, there was no way
we could afford secretarial staff. We all had to do our own support work. The computer made that possible. Now, I don't
leave home without one tucked under my arm, and I always
bring along my notebook computer to a business planning retreat.

On the eve of a business planning session not long ago, I
found myself alone with the president of my client's company
at the cabin we would be using for the next several days. Before hitting the hay, I got out my computer to show him a
game that I had bought for $5 at an airport news stand. The
game involves finding hidden treasure and escaping from a
complex maze.

The president— a fellow who has evidently spoken out in
opposition to a computer purchase or two in his day— was

amazed at how much fun it was. He got the hang of it in the first five minutes, and I saw how quickly playing a simple game could overcome a fear of computers. Maybe all of the die-hards who still haven't learned how to use a computer should start by playing one of these games. I bet my client will be more willing to see what can be done with a computer now that he has controlled one successfully.

Creative Promotion— We recently received a great little piece of direct mail from Rizzo Associates, Inc. (Natick, MA), a 120-person engineering and environmental consulting firm located right down the street from us. The purpose of the brochure was to announce the firm's Employee Stock Ownership Plan (ESOP), but it used a creative approach.

"Call us," it read. "One of our owners would like to work with you on your next project." And printed in small, white letters in the background of the text was the name of every employee in the firm. This piece is going to send a strong message to clients and potential clients that Rizzo has some significant staff capabilities. Hats off to them for doing something creative to announce their ESOP, instead of walking right past a great P.R. opportunity, like so many other firms in this business would have done. **Z**

D E T A I L S
. . . .

QUOTABLE: "For years the National Science Foundation was saying by the year 2000 or 2005 we'd experience a real shortage of design engineering talent, but it doesn't exist.

"They based their research on a number of findings like the number of engineering students graduating from college and foreign nationals they expected to return to their home nations. But since the studies, we experienced an end to the Cold War and the downsizing of America's military budget."

SOURCE: Laura Mackail, executive director of the National Technical Services Association (Alexandria, VA), an organization of companies that place temporary technical workers.

■

HELP STAFF WORK HARDER: Firms will spend thousands to relocate professionals from Alaska to Alabama, but they may get a much bigger productivity gain for a fraction of the cost by moving staffers from one town to the next.

Are some of your professional employees commuting 30, or 45, or 60 or more minutes each way to work? Why not offer to move them closer to the office and reduce that commute to 20 minutes or five minutes? Or how about a bonus for relocating within a certain distance of the office?

Not only is it a benefit to employees (more convenient, less wear and tear on the car), they're bound to put in more hours on the job, whether it's staying a half hour later to get a proposal out or stopping in for a little while on Sunday afternoon to get ready for the week.

Be sure to consult a labor attorney knowledgeable in federal, state, and local laws on how this policy should be worded.

■

DESIGN/BUILD MAKING INROADS?: Design-build is five times more likely to be the project delivery method in certain utility and industrial projects than in water/sewer or road/bridge projects, according to a report by the F.W. Dodge Division of McGraw Hill and the Design-Build Institute of America. The report analyzed the percentage of contract awards of $5 million and over from April 1993 to April 1994 that were design-build projects. Five percent of power/communication utilities projects and 4% of industrial plants were design-build jobs, compared with 1% of water/sewer projects and less than 1% of road/bridge projects.

■

Rewarding non-managers

OVER the years, principals at Sherlock, Smith & Adams, Inc. (Montgomery, AL), a 70-person A/E firm, refined the company's incentive bonus program to better reflect non-management employees' contribution to the firm's success.

"Instead of, say, a clean work space or dressing professionally, we take into account things like how someone deals with a client in crisis," says Roland Vaughan, the firm's president.

He's right. But how do you devise a bonus system for non-managers that works? Start by asking *why* you give bonuses. It's to reward employees for past good deeds and to provide an incentive for future ones. With this in mind, any system that *doesn't* single out and reward past performance and *doesn't* show employees what they need to do to receive future reward is bound to fail. Here's our advice:

Set bonus pools based on the profitability of the employee's group and the overall firm. NBBJ (Seattle, WA), a 200-person architectural firm, divides its employees into discipline "studios," each with an annual goal. The bonus money each studio receives depends on the firm's profitability and the percentage of its goal a studio meets. The money is then divided among the studio's individuals at the discretion of four management-level studio leaders.

Allow each manager to divide the bonus pool for his or her group. The distribution should be based on the manager's evaluation of an employee's performance. And it needs to be the manager who *knows* what that person has really done. At the same time, make sure people doing evaluations use the same yardstick and give sufficient effort to the task. Professionals in our industry are notorious for giving this duty short shrift. Vaughan says his firm requires managers who conduct performance reviews to justify those that are above average or below average, ensuring more thought goes into the process.

Let employees track their progress. If a bonus plan is to succeed, employees *must* be able to understand and figure out the criteria by which they are being judged, and what percent of the bonus pool they'll receive if they meet their goals. This means sharing financial information with *all* staff. A good test— if employees are *surprised* (whether pleasantly or unpleasantly) by the amount of their bonuses, something is wrong.

"Everyone in the studio knows how the firm is performing, how the bonus pool is doing, how the studio is doing, and how much the studio gets," says NBBJ CEO James Jonassen. "If people don't get much, they know they didn't get much relative to what was available. Then we can talk about it."

Distribute bonuses more than once a year. The motivating power of money is short-lived. Rewards are most effective if they're given at least quarterly, or even monthly. "Christmas bonuses don't work," points out Bill Aden, CEO of Draper Aden Associates (Blacksburg, VA), a 92-person consulting engineering and environmental firm.

Give high performers significantly higher bonuses than low performers. On the other hand, giving *no* bonus to someone when times are good is probably overly harsh. If the employee is not contributing, why is he or she on the payroll? Vaughan is proud that his system has not only helped reward those truly deserving, but has increased the productivity of some low-performing employees by identifying their problems. Those who couldn't improve are gone, he adds.

Give bonuses to some people even when the firm *isn't* profitable. Staff people have much less control than management over the firm's performance. Don't let the extraordinary efforts of individuals go unrecognized.

Making a bonus system work is not easy. It's always *easier* to spread the rewards evenly so no one will cry foul. But any system that works is going to make *some* people unhappy and motivate them to change their ways. **Z**

D E T A I L S

▪ ▪ ▪ ▪ ▪ ▪ ▪ ▪ ▪ ▪ ▪ ▪ ▪ ▪ ▪ ▪ ▪ ▪ ▪

BENEFITS QUIZ: Employee benefits are a no-win situation for the average design firm. On the one hand, they rarely help you in hiring or motivating staff. On the other hand, they can create big headaches when not handled properly and fairly.

A/E/P and environmental consulting firms in general can be proud of the decent package of benefits they offer. A few firms even offer extraordinary benefits.

Where does your firm rank? Take this test. Give yourself one point for each benefit your firm provides to *all* staff (except where noted in parentheses):

___Health insurance (1 pt. if employee contributes to premium; 2 pts. if company pays all premium)

___Dental insurance

___Long-term disability insurance

___Vacation (minimum two weeks for full-time employees)

___Holidays (1 pt. for 1-8 holidays, 2 pts. for 9 or more)

___Pension, 401(k), or other retirement plan.

___Flex time

___Free coffee (Subtract 1 pt. if staff must chip in for coffee)

___Free beverages (other than coffee)

___Free parking (1 pt. only if office in urban area)

___Tuition reimbursement for job-related courses

___Sporting or cultural events tickets (available to all staff)

___Holiday party

___Company picnic

___Health club membership

___TOTAL POINTS

Scores— 1-5: Even Bob Cratchit got a day off. 6-10: You're about average. 11+: Maybe you need to learn to say no.

▪

IF YOU'RE TRYING to find low-cost ways to reward employees while simultaneously educating them, try this approach offered by Bob Maxman, COO at Jones, Edmunds & Associates, Inc. (Gainesville, FL), a 90-person consulting engineering firm. His company buys lunch once a week for about 25-30 engineers and scientists, where they talk about a subject or two. Recent topics have included ways to do proposals, what to do on a construction site, and what the construction services group does. "I try to keep it from being a lecture," says Maxman.

▪

Secrets of success

I T DRIVES me crazy when people say you can't make any money in the A/E (or architecture, or environmental consulting, or whatever) business— especially when the person talking is a firm *principal.*

Although that's been the experience of many principals, you and the others in your firm can do *plenty* well in this business. I know (from our annual *Principal's Survey*) that the typical principal earns, in a good year, around $100,000. But there are lots of people making $200,000, $300,000, even $500,000 per year— or more— and doing it consistently. And don't think that all of these people are sole proprietors, or one of two partners in a firm.

Every so often I like to consider what makes these people so successful. Here's some of what I am seeing that sets the really successful principals apart from the pack:

1. **Super-successful principals have a knack for making other people *like* them, both inside and outside of their firms.** You never know when you'll need the help of a friend, and you can't have too many of them. Whether it's a fellow principal whose support you need to get elected to the board of directors, or someone you can call in a client organization to help get your check in the mail, the big money-makers in this business realize how

important friendships are, and make friends everywhere they go.

2. **Successful principals don't feel the need to do everything themselves and are good delegators.** A lot of the engineers, architects, and scientists I know who get to the principal level do so because they are good at what they do— sometimes *too* good. They tend to be perfectionists. As a result, they don't want to dole out work to other people because they can always do it better. No doubt that's true— at *first*. But in the long run, you've got to develop other people. They won't learn unless you give them a chance. Quality or service could actually suffer at first, but eventually the firm may be better off for it. Successful people realize they have to part with certain tasks so they can concentrate on what's most beneficial to the *firm*.

3. **Successful principals are human and they know it.** Being "human" means that you have compassion for other people. You have to be sympathetic to your loyal employees' problems and needs. Being human also means that you have to be in touch with your *own* needs, such as the need to spend time with your family, the need to exercise to stay healthy, and the need for a break every once in a while. Successful principals work hard at work and play hard at play. They have balance.

4. **Successful principals have a good awareness of what's going on in the world, the local community, and their clients' businesses.** To really succeed in this business, you have to be able to deal with the highest-level people in your clients' organizations. The highest-level people in any organization, public or private, tend to be the smarter ones. They are multi-dimensional people with a wide range of interests. They are staying up with what is going on. Instead of watching "Roseanne," they may be reading *Zen and the Art of Motorcycle Maintenance*. You have to be multi-dimensional, too.

5. **Successful principals have the "killer instinct."** I've seen some principals cringe at this notion— being a "killer" to them means being immoral or unethical in some way. But to the really successful principal, all the "killer instinct" means is having a strong desire to win. And in order to win, you have to beat the competition. Everything is *not* okay if you don't win the job. It means that having a 20%, or 30%, or even 60% success rate in the pursuit of new projects simply isn't good enough.

6. **Finally, the most successful principals work in successful firms, ones that are willing to invest.** You can have a good year and make a lot of money in the design business. A number of our clients did that last year. But we believe to do that *every* year, you have to invest in the business, and spend money on computers, facilities, support systems, training, development of standards, and so forth. You can't eat the entire crop after every harvest— you've got to save some seed for next year. **Z**

D E T A I L S
· ·

A/E/P and environmental consulting firm principals are a consistent bunch. They work about 50 hours a week, earn more vacation than they use, get (and stay) married, like American-made cars, and are friends with their fellow principals.

These characteristics are, of course, stereotypes. But they're not unfounded. They have been culled from three separate editions of Mark Zweig & Associates' *Principal's Survey of A/E/P & Environmental Consulting Firms*. And though many aspects of being a principal change little from year to year, the survey also looks at some of the elements that *have* changed. Here's a look:

Cellular telephones. In 1994, nearly two-thirds of all principals in the survey had a car phone. This number has grown by 58% since 1991.

"I think it has become almost essential," says Michael Davy, P.E., president of 50-employee civil engineering firm Davy Engineering Company, Inc. (LaCrosse, WI). "I probably spend three to four hours a week on the phone in the car. That's time that otherwise I would have to spend in the office returning calls."

Computer use. This is another aspect that has changed dramatically in the past several years. The number of principals who have a computer on their desk grew from 46% in 1991 to 63% in 1994. Of course, some of these computer-literate principals are working in small firms and need to stay involved in production.

Age is a factor in computer usage among principals. Only 54% of principals 49 years old or older had a computer on their desk, as opposed to 73% of those 48 or younger. As septuagenarian Leslie N. Boney, Jr., chairman of 40-employee Boney Architects, Inc. (Wilmington, NC) says, "I haven't found it necessary to learn it at my ripe old age."

Compensation. The *Principal's Survey* also shows compensation figures lagging behind the Consumer Price Index. Though inflation grew by only 3% in 1993, total compensation grew by an even slower 2%.

This was no surprise to Gary Van Wieringen, president of Entranco Engineers, Inc. (Bellevue, WA), a 100-employee civil engineering firm. He says his salary in 1994 will probably be 25% *less* than it was three years ago. This reflects the marketplace, says Van Wieringen. "I do think I see the industry beginning to pick up again, but that's probably six to nine months away," he says.

Not all firm principals are taking pay cuts, but many remain cautious. Increased competition and the recession took their toll on the profitability of many companies, including 45-person A/E firm, Gordon H. Chong & Associates, Inc. (San Francisco, CA). "We are oriented towards stabilizing salaries, but increasing total compensation through incentive," says firm president Gordon Chong, FAIA.

■

Selling

TWENTY contacts per month! To know why we have a problem selling services in the A/E/P and environmental consulting business, look no further than the goals we lay out for our marketing and business development people.

According to our research, only 15% of business development reps and 13% of marketing directors even *have* contact goals, and when they do, the median number is only 20 contacts per month! (SOURCE: 1994 Mark Zweig & Associates *Marketing Survey of A/E/P and Environmental Consulting Firms*)

That number blows my mind. I can remember making 50 or more calls in less than four hours as a young marketer in this business. Twenty contacts per month is ridiculous—that's only 240 in a year! *No one* can be effective with those kinds of probabilities working against them. It's time we get back to the basics of selling or we deserve to go out of business. Here's my advice:

1. **Enter the client firm at the highest level.** One of the classic mistakes made by marketers in our industry is that they don't call on the right people. They call on people who are *easy* to talk with, or people they've talked with *before*, or anyone who *will* talk with them. The *best* way to sell is to get to the person at the top of the organi-

zation. He or she can push you down to those lower in the hierarchy, but rarely can you go the other way.

2. **Make lots of calls.** One of the best educational experiences I ever had was working as a graduate assistant for a marketing research professor. I learned all about probability theory. This was reinforced when I started selling. I knew that the probabilities were only 40% that I could get through to someone and about 30% that he or she would have a possible need for my services and agree to see me. I then knew that I had at least a 20% shot at getting the job. Experienced sellers of anything know exactly what their success rate is and know that every call they make, whether it results in a sale or not, takes them closer to hitting their goal. The *probabilities* take care of them. That's why 20 calls a month isn't enough!

3. **Practice makes perfect.** Whether it's tennis, carpentry, water colors, or selling, you're bound to get better if you *practice.* Someone who makes 100 calls a month is getting *five* times the experience of someone who makes only 20. The person getting five times the practice will probably be comfortable with selling sooner and be more effective at it than the other person.

4. **Selling is a sequential process.** Too many people seem to forget that selling is a step-by-step, sequential process and are disappointed if they don't make a sale right out of the chute. It's just like learning how to walk. First you creep, then you crawl, then you stand and hold on to things, then you walk unassisted. Selling works the same way. Very rarely will someone buy something from you on the first contact. When making cold calls, your goal should be to determine if a need exists or not and set up the next contact. Once a need is identified, your goal should be to get together with the client to talk and perhaps see the situation first-hand. The next step is to have the opportunity to make the client a proposal. The final step is closing the sale. Rarely do you go from meeting the client directly to closing— all of the steps in the

process need to be followed. Experienced sellers simply try to keep their clients in the process. As long as the client doesn't say no, they keep moving them on to the next step.

5. **Not everyone is good at selling.** The fact is that some people have the ability to sell and others do not. I'm not sure it can be taught. We have a hard time with that concept in our business. Since we want all of our employees to be successful, we push people into roles they have no interest in or aptitude for. Selling is one of those roles, since the sellers usually get the most recognition in the typical A/E/P or environmental firm. Everyone deserves a chance to sell if they want it, but not everyone will be good at it.

6. **Sell when business is good— not just when business is bad.** Last, and perhaps most importantly, is the concept that "when you're hot, you're hot, and when you're not, you're not." Applied to a selling context, this means that when you have lots of work is the *best* time to be out selling. Your confidence will come through, you'll negotiate a better fee, and you'll have a lot more fun doing it than when you really *need* the work. Desperation always shines through! **z**

D E T A I L S

· · · · · · · · · · · · · · · · · · · ·

ELEVEN SELLING SECRETS: Want to improve your selling ability? Try these 11 tips:

1. Keep the firm's size small enough that you always have more possibilities for work coming in than you can do. That way, you won't get ripped off on your fee.

2. Carry a notebook/laptop computer and portable ink jet printer so you can put together a proposal or contract at the client's office on request.

3. Never make fewer than 10 marketing-related phone calls in a row because you won't be warmed up until you are through with the first five.

4. When telephone prospecting, remember that your goal is to identify a need and set up the next contact. You probably won't get hired over the telephone!

5. Never send out a brochure in advance of a sales call. Give it to the client afterward, or better yet, walk him or her through it personally at the end of your visit.

6. Always talk to the highest-level decision-maker that you can get through to in the potential client organization.

7. Existing and former clients are your best prospects.

8. Make sure you have identified and contacted every possible local buyer of the services that your firm provides before chasing after clients or projects out of your area.

9. Don't allow the client to focus on the cost of your services. Instead, move the discussion to the cost of the completed project, the cost of the facility over time, or the cost of not dealing with the problem properly.

10. Remember that activity precedes results. If outgoing telephone calls and personal visits to clients are down, incoming leads are down, and proposal volume is down, anticipate a future sales slowdown, even if it is currently at a peak.

11. Be desirable, but hard to get.

■

QUOTABLE: "Engineers are great with numbers... until you put a dollar sign in front of them."

SOURCE: A couple of frustrated financial managers of a major design firm (who asked to remain anonymous).

■

QUOTABLE: "In smaller firms such as mine, the president is going to have to be billable, otherwise the company can't afford him. You don't get all those perks from the tooth fairy."

Philip Corlew, president and CEO of M.B. Corlew & Associates, Inc. (Edwardsville, IL), a 16-person consulting engineering firm.

■

Service life cycle

DO YOU KNOW where you are in the "life cycle" for each of your firm's services? If not, you should. What you learn can have profound implications for everything the company does.

There are four (and sometimes five) stages to any service life cycle— the Introductory Stage, the Growth Stage, the Maturity Stage, the Decline Stage, and, optionally, the Rebirth Stage.

The *Introductory Stage* is where a new service is invented. At this stage, the biggest issue is simply convincing clients they have a need. Once they are convinced, they'll probably buy the service from the first firm that can fill the need. For example, the client may be unaware of new requirements affecting lead paint abatement, or that roofing consultants have a whole new way of dealing with leaky roofs. Firms with services in the introductory stage must educate their potential clients. The total market for services in the Introductory Stage is not very large, though it may have a lot of potential.

In the *Growth Stage*, more service-provider firms enter the market, but the market may be growing so quickly that demand still outstrips supply. Billing multiples are typically strong in this stage, as are profits of firms supplying the service to the marketplace. In the Growth Stage, the important factor is technical capability to provide the service. The fact that a service provider may not have worked for boat loads of clients similar to the one at hand is not usually an issue.

By the time the service enters the **Maturity Stage**, new competition has entered the market to the point where supply finally catches up with demand. Prices are driven downward. It becomes much harder for new competitors to enter the market because so many experienced players are already in it. Now knowledge of the client type and location of the service provider drives the selection process, since technical capability is widespread. This is where the bulk of services provided by A/E, consulting engineering, and even environmental consulting firms are today.

The fourth stage is the **Decline Stage**, which services such as asbestos abatement have already entered. Once almost all the asbestos is out of buildings, which it will eventually be (assuming it's not still being used, as it is in some foreign countries), the overall asbestos abatement market will shrink. Competition becomes even more intense and fees are driven downward, as supply far outstrips demand.

Sometimes service markets are reborn when the level of competition drops along with the pricing structure during the Decline Stage. Some competitors price themselves out of business. Others move onto new markets because they can't make any money in the service anymore. Eventually equilibrium between supply and demand is again established. In some cases, the service market is reborn, and may go back into maturity or even growth. **Rebirth** is the fifth stage in the service life cycle.

Where do the services that your firm provides fall in the market life cycle? Keep developing new services that have a strong growth potential. For services in the Maturity Stage, look for ways to differentiate your firm's offerings with specialized client/industry knowledge. For services in the Decline Stage, don't overlook the potential for rebirth. **z**

Support staff

I HEAR from many disgruntled people working in support roles in A/E and environmental consulting firms— ("support" meaning anyone whose primary job does not create revenue for the firm). I know how they feel. I was one of them once.

These people are in high-placed roles such as chief financial officer and director of marketing, down to positions such as file clerk or print room operator. The plight of the support person is a common morale problem in A/E and environmental firms, and it won't go away just because we want it to. We have to confront it head on.

What's the problem? A lot of people will say that those in support roles don't *earn* as much as their technical counterparts. But the truth is, there are many who do. Some even make more. So what are they complaining about? I think you'll find they have three real gripes—lack of prestige, lack of ownership opportunities, and lack of job security.

Too many professional service firms treat support staff like second-class citizens. They give the support people the hand-me-down computers, when the technical staff get the latest equipment. Lower status administrative support staffers often sit in the worst office space— usually a cramped cubicle in a high traffic area with virtually no layout space and no windows. And higher status support people, such as the

CFO, may not get a company vehicle or sit on the firm's board of directors, whereas someone else at their level in the hierarchy would. It's *really* demeaning when someone with the title of "marketing director" is excluded from the business planning process or retreat— something we see quite often.

Ownership in a closely held firm is another sore point. Many privately held firms exclude support staff from consideration as owners or partners (outside of an ESOP). Most of us in the know have to admit that equates to a lack of clout in the typical professional service firm.

Lack of job security happens because when there's a dip in workload or the financial picture isn't as rosy as it should be, the first place many firms look to cut is the support staff.

I understand *why* these things happen. In *any* organization— and A/E and environmental consulting firms are certainly no exception— those who produce the revenue are ostensibly more valuable to the firm than those who just figure out how to *save* or *spend* money. I know I never wanted to hear that when I worked in a support role— I always justified my keep by how much money the company saved from having me there— but saving money is not where the real action is. Practically anyone can figure out how to save money— the real key is figuring out how to make it.

There is *some* truth to the old adage technical and professional people are fond of: "If we weren't here, you wouldn't have a job." On the other hand, there are many arguments against that thinking:

1. **Many of those who are designated support actually *are* revenue generators.** I have seen many secretaries, word processors and blueprint operators charging the bulk of their time to billable projects. I have also seen many marketing people filling the role of P.I.C. to make sure the client is happy.

2. **Good marketing, human resources, and finance and accounting directors are worth their weight in gold.** On a number of occasions, I have seen the top finance or accounting person literally *save* the firm by increasing cash

flow when the company needed it to stay in business. Yet, they rarely got the credit they deserved. I have seen similar instances with both marketing and human resources people— where their actions had a major impact on the firm's ability to prosper far beyond the short term.

3. **The negative ramifications of treating support people like second-class citizens outweigh the costs of treating them like everybody else.** Including someone in a meeting, getting them a new desk chair, or putting them in a window slot often doesn't cost you much, yet it may pay big dividends in terms of morale and productivity.

The bottom line is everyone is important. If your attitude is that support people are less important than your technical staff and are easy to replace, you'll be spending plenty of time defusing morale problems, interviewing job candidates, and listening to the gripes of your technical people who really need the help. If, on the other hand, you treat your support staff like *you* want to be treated, you'll likely be rewarded with a well-oiled machine that functions as a super production *and* profit generator. **Z**

D E T A I L S

■ ■ ■ ■ ■ ■ ■ ■ ■ ■ ■ ■ ■ ■ ■ ■ ■ ■ ■

OUR FREQUENT criticism of paying overtime to exempt professionals prompted a response from David Evans, CEO of David Evans & Associates, Inc. (Portland, OR), a 500-person consulting engineering firm.

"People working for any company or corporation should get paid for their efforts," writes Evans. "Anything less than pay for work is a blatant statement that the efforts performed or the skill, education, and dedication of your staff are not fully valued... The argument that 'overtime' pay becomes expected and is often abused, suggests that our professionals can't be trusted.

"If your staff can't be trusted to work diligently for 45 hours, how can you trust them to work 40 hours? Relegating professionals to piece workers is one of the reasons our profession doesn't garner the respect it deserves."

■

OVERTIME ADVICE: Mark A. Casso, general counsel for the American Consulting Engineers Council (Washington, DC), says the Fair Labor Standards Act is outdated.

The law is in a state of flux, Casso says, because it was established 56 years ago when manufacturing drove the nation's economy. Now, in service industries like consulting engineering, architecture, and environmental consulting, the commodity is the professional, not a tangible product.

That disparity has forced courts to often *interpret* the intent of the law. And those interpretations have varied widely, Casso says. "It pre-sents a potential problem because people are looking for black and white answers, and there are none," he says.

Since hourly workers *must* be paid time-and-a-half for overtime, a court ruling that removes the "exempt" status for a salaried employee can be extremely costly to a firm, as in the recent decision against Malcolm Pirnie, Inc. (White Plains, NY), a 2,000-person environmental firm.

At the beginning of 1994, two bills were being considered by Congress that would amend the law and make it more realistic, Casso says. Meanwhile, some of the issues that have been used to determine hourly versus salaried employees are overtime pay, fixed schedules, time sheets, and paid leave. Here are Casso's suggestions:

■ Use separate checks for extra compensation to salaried workers.

■ Pay it monthly or quarterly, not weekly.

■ Call it a bonus, not overtime.

■ Base bonuses on factors like timely performance, level of effort, or client satisfaction, not only extra hours worked.

■ Don't set a fixed schedule or minimum number of hours for salaried employees.

■ Require time sheets only to track hours for billing purposes, and call them something other than time sheets.

■

The four functions of management

MOST A/E/P and environmental consulting firm insiders would agree that we, as a group of companies, do not *manage* very well. I say that because if we did, we would not be an industry made up of 69,000 firms, averaging only 10-15 employees each.

My thoughts keep going back to the time-tested definition of management and its four functions— *planning, leading, organizing,* and *controlling.* My conclusion is that we do a terrible job with the first three functions (planning, leading, and organizing), and over-emphasize the last (controlling).

But why is that? The uninitiated would think that design and technical professionals would be great at this stuff. We have to do it for our clients— why can't we do it for ourselves? Here are my thoughts:

We don't *plan* because it's not fun. People tend to do what they enjoy— and engineers, architects, planners, and scientists are no exception. Most design professionals would rather be *doing* than *planning.* We have no tolerance for the ambiguity of the planning process, and no faith that it works anyway. Planning takes you out of the problem-solving mode, and reduces the excitement that comes from being in a crisis and solving it. Putting yourself into a dangerous situation and surviving can be addictive. Why else would people sky-dive or bungee jump?

We don't *lead* because we feel there is something inherently wrong with doing so. Many people running professional service firms today started out not as entrepreneurs, but as model employees. The result is that when they eventually phase into ownership/management positions, it may take a while for them to become leaders instead of followers. Many of them were programmed in the early stages of their professional career to distrust management— to think that management regularly misleads or manipulates them. And if you look around, you'll see there are some good reasons for this thinking. One of our competitors advised firms in his newsletter to tell project team members that the project budget is smaller than it actually is to improve profitability! So much for building trust between management and employees.

We don't *organize* because we are preoccupied with the present. We don't organize for the same reasons we don't plan. Organization requires us to take time away from current activities to better prepare ourselves for future work. But the pressures most managers in professional service firms face to stay job-chargeable, minimize overhead, and get out and sell also keep us out of this "organization" thing. As a group, we are so focused on survival that we systematically chip away at our firms' futures.

We overemphasize *control* because it's familiar (and therefore feels safe). This is one function of management that most of us will heartily acknowledge our belief in— control. As managers, we have to check on the work of others; make the final decisions on all important matters; decide what information goes out to the project team members, discipline heads, or even our fellow principals; determine who gets how much of a raise or bonus, even for those employees we may not recognize if we saw them on the street; and so on. The result of this constant overemphasis on control is that we don't develop any managers who can get us out of the position where we need to control. It's a vicious cycle.

So how can we improve our managers' abilities to plan, lead, and organize, and reduce their tendencies to control?

1. **Force planning.** No one will do it unless you insist on it. Force your managers to plan their activities, to look ahead, to anticipate what they will do about problems before they occur. Show your people how to plan. Tell them what you want their plans to look like. Don't let them off the hook on planning.

2. **Support leadership initiatives.** Many A/E/P and environmental firms are set up to systematically run off those who have the most leadership potential. Recognize who your leaders are and encourage them by first giving them the opportunity to lead, and second, by supporting their attempts to do so. Don't put them down for taking initiative. Don't label anyone who wants to lead others as "power crazed." Don't make your natural-born leaders go through the same steps to move up as those who lack the requisite personality and mental attributes.

3. **Get organized yourself.** If you want your people to be organized, *you* have to be organized. That means you don't forget appointments, you get the meeting notes out as soon as the meeting is over, you don't lose things people send you, and you have an office that doesn't look like the paper section of the neighborhood recycling center. Think about it.

4. Give up control and sell the benefits of doing so to your second tier. People at the top set the example for how things are done. I've seen so many CEOs who are still doing first-level technical work. If you are like that, your staff will be, too. You have to delegate everything you can. And you have to keep telling your managers that they should be doing the same thing. Because if they don't part with some of the control, they will never be able to get out of their current mode and into one that has a bigger impact on the company. And that's where we all know the biggest share of financial (and psychological) rewards are! **Z**

D E T A I L S

. . . .

PROFILES OF SUCCESSFUL LEADERS:

I consider myself really fortunate to have as clients and friends some really great leaders. You may not see all of these people on the cover of *Inc.* magazine, but that doesn't mean they don't have a unique blend of personal attributes that makes other people want to follow them into battle. Some of these include:

■ The ability to set priorities. I have yet to see a truly effective leader who doesn't have superior ability to prioritize. Let's face it. The A/E/P and environmental businesses offer many opportunities for someone to get sidetracked if they are inclined to do so. The phone rings all day. The in-box fills up. The mail comes in. And everyone has a problem they need your help with. The ability to decide what's most critical is key to success as a leader.

■ A super high energy level. The best leaders I know in this business are all people who work a lot, move fast, and do lots of things at once. They all have an energy level that stands out as extraordinary. This cuts across all age categories of leaders, too.

■ Passion for their work. Show me someone who feels there is a higher purpose for their work, and I'll show you someone who gets a lot done in spite of obstacles. The best leaders I know of pursue their mission with a zeal and enthusiasm that just has to be contagious to those that work for them. It's really essential to sustaining their own motivation over time.

■ A big picture vision that is grounded in reality. There are a lot of people out there who fancy themselves as "big picture" thinkers, but who cannot ever seem to get anything done. Likewise, there are those who pride themselves on telling you why something won't work— who find fault with anything new. The best leaders are people who can distinguish what ideas will take the company where it wants to go in the long run, yet are practical and implementable today.

■ Outstanding communication skills. Good leaders realize that if others are to follow, they have to be able to communicate their mission, their vision, their goals, their enthusiasm, and their passion. This requires them to be effective speakers, both one-on-one and in a group. It may also require them to be effective writers so they can reach others they won't be interacting with personally.

■

212

Typical architect? (we hope not)

WE RECENTLY had the experience of working with an architect. Business has been good, and we are committed to growth, so we decided to triple our office space by moving to a new suite right here in our same building.

Our building complex had just the right size space we needed. Unfortunately, it had been poorly carved off from another, larger space. This required an all-new main entrance and reception area, as well as an additional emergency entrance to meet local building codes. On top of this, we planned to add a new conference room and an employee exercise room (maybe if it's convenient, I'll get off my rear end and exercise!).

We made up a preliminary plan showing how we thought things ought to look, and the landlords sent it on to their architects. The next thing we know, before we have signed the lease or ever even seen the plan, it's being put out to bid. The problem was the contractors were bidding on things we didn't want.

For example, the architect decided to nearly double the width of our conference room (from 13 to approximately 25 feet). Her change required that a partition be installed bridging a window— but the best part was that if you wanted to get to the workroom where all of our book and newsletter orders are processed (which doubles as a utility area with special HVAC and electrical equipment), you would have to go through the conference room! That really made sense!

The reception area, too, was modified for no apparent reason. Instead of a 10x8 foot space off of the waiting area where the receptionist's desk and credenza were to be located, we ended up with an 8x3 area too small to do anything with.

A glass partition for the new exercise room was being tossed out instead of reused alongside the other glass interior partitions for that room. The plans noted that existing carpeting was being re-used, and that we wanted an all-new 2x2 ceiling put in. What we wanted, however, was all-new *carpeting* and to re-use the *existing* ceiling!

When we found out from the building superintendent that bids were being taken for these improvements, we told him to stop until we had a decent set of plans and specifications to work from. We completed negotiations on our deal with the landlord, which included the landlord paying for one revision of the plans and specs. We then set up a meeting with the architect— an associate in a prominent firm.

After she arrived 20 minutes late with no explanation, we sat down to talk about what we wanted done. She asked what we did for a living but showed no acknowledgment that it was in any way connected to her business— we might as well have been dry cleaners for all she cared. After we sat down in my office, she first argued with me about what the width of the conference room would be if we put the wall where we wanted it. She was wrong. Then I asked her which was cheaper— to put in an all-glass interior partition or a six-foot wall with glass (or glass block) to the ceiling. She wouldn't give me a straight answer, and instead tried to talk me into a full floor-to-ceiling panel next to the door only.

Then we talked about the ceiling. I asked for a ball-park price per square foot for a new 2x2 ceiling to be installed in the event we did want to consider that option, and she couldn't provide me with any idea of what that would cost, either. She said she wasn't used to dealing with the cost of things— that was strictly the domain of the contractor.

You can imagine how much fun we had talking about how to re-use that glass interior partition for the exercise room. It took us 10 minutes of talking to come to the conclusion that we could use what was there the way we wanted to.

Finally, we were unable to get a specific date for when our plans would be finished before she left. She wasn't angry or upset with us— I really think that this woman was simply incapable of giving anyone a definite answer to a question.

Hopefully, our experience wasn't typical of what most clients of design firms are going through. If this kind of communication ability is the norm for an associate level staffer in one of our readers' firms, we've got some big problems in this industry. It makes it easier to understand why so many A/E firms feel threatened by design-build. **Z**

D E T A I L S

. . . .

OUR FRUSTRATIONS with the architect designing our new offices at the beginning of 1994 (see preceding article) inspired several readers— most of them architects— to comment.

"Your mistake was letting the landlord hire the architect," says G. Milton Small, principal at Small Kane Architects (Raleigh, NC), a 14-person architectural firm. "Landlords provide 'free' design services, so the tenant thinks he's getting something for nothing. But you usually get what you pay for."

Small says the architect's allegiance *must* be with the person who does the hiring, in this case the landlord. "Not many designers, or other professionals, can balance two masters and do the job they should. You need to have somebody who's your advocate."

■

QUOTABLE: "One of the biggest complaints i hear about architects is that they don't listen. That's some people's perception of architects. Yes, they go to the meetings, then they go back to their office and do what they think is right. We're the experts, but we have to remember the client brings the value to the table. He knows what he wants."

SOURCE: John Knight, architect and vice president of Robert and Company (Atlanta, GA).

■

CONSTRUCTION MEANS/METHODS: Design professionals have been taught the construction contractor alone is responsible for construction means, methods, techniques,

sequences, and procedures. Standard design contracts support this.

But design professionals *do* become involved in construction means/methods. David Hatem, a partner at law firm Burns & Levinson (Boston, MA), offers this advice for the design professional of record.

1. Your contract documents should require the contractor to retain a qualified designer to prepare design, drawings, and specs related to means/methods.

2. Even if you don't have contractual responsibility for reviewing construction means/methods, you may *become* responsible by actual conduct. If possible, refuse to get involved.

3. If you *do* get involved in means/methods issues, be aware of an increased risk of liability, particularly if it creates ambiguity about the roles and responsibilities of contractor and designer.

4. If, during negotiations, you think you might have to get involved in means/methods issues, spell out the nature and extent of your involvement in the agreement.

5. If you can't foresee it and it comes up later, require an amendment to the agreement.

For the designer of record, getting involved in construction means/methods should be the *exception*, not the rule, says Hatem. Finally, expect to get paid for the increased effort and liability you face when you do get involved.

■

Understanding what motivates

WHAT IS the best way to motivate staff? When faced
with that question, most firm principals think
about what to *give* them. The experts tell us to pay
spot bonuses for an effort that goes above and beyond the
call of duty, or promote our committed folks that we can't yet
make principals to "senior associate," or start a special "employee of the year" award, which is announced at the holiday
party.

While I certainly wouldn't deny that your employees may
expect you to do some of these things, and that sometimes
they may be necessary, I don't think they really address the
motivation issue.

If you really want to motivate, you may not want to *give*
anything. *Offering* may get you a lot more than *giving* does.
What do I mean by that?

Offer a challenge. A/E/P and environmental firms are,
by and large, run by and staffed with intelligent people who
like to test the limits of their abilities. They want to be
stretched by trying new things that they may not necessarily
have the qualifications to do. Any firm that wants motivated
people has to address this need, while providing enough supervision and guidance to put out acceptable quality.

Offer work that the person can't get elsewhere. This is one of the keys to growing a professional service business. If you want to attract and motivate the best and brightest people, you have to offer work that they could not get on their own or at another firm. This may mean bigger projects, or projects that require many different professional or technical skills and talents that another firm may not have.

Offer the opportunity to get a pay increase or bonus based on job performance. This is in contrast to giving cost-of-living raises, or paying out bonuses based on the employee's position in the firm's hierarchy. It also conflicts with having position grades and associated salary brackets. Although some employees no doubt want this kind of bureaucracy, it is this kind of nonsense that demoralizes the best staff by effectively capping opportunities.

Offer the opportunity to learn this *business*. A/E/P and environmental firms often forget that they are in the *consulting* business— not a technical service business. People who work in the firm need to have more than just technical or design skills to succeed. Developing these skills builds confidence and motivation. Not developing these skills hurts confidence and reduces an employee's willingness to work. All employees need to understand the overall business. It affects everything they do in their technical work. And they won't learn it if you keep them insulated from client contact, proposal writing, project development, and firm financial information.

Offer the opportunity to move up by bypassing the established career path. I'm not saying that there shouldn't be an established order of steps to go through to become a project manager or principal. But there also ought to be a way to make exceptions to that order for someone who clearly has the capability to move up faster. Although most would never admit it, too many A/E/P firms operate on a seniority basis. Forcing everyone into the same mold is not the way to motivate your best and brightest— they should be able to move up the ladder faster than someone with fewer career options.

Offer the opportunity for your staff to grow personally. This means you have to give the employee feedback, and it probably won't always be positive. Most managers don't like giving bad news, so they avoid it, doing a tremendous disservice to their employees in the process. The highly motivated employee appreciates tactfully delivered feedback that will help his or her career. Getting no feedback is de-motivating to somebody who really wants to be good at what he or she does, and wants to be rewarded for it.

Offer the opportunity to get an entrepreneurial experience. Some— not all— architects, engineers, planners and scientists eventually get bored with technical or design work, or even project management. They may become dissatisfied with the rewards, both psychological and monetary, that they can earn in those roles, and long for a different experience that only ownership can provide. That's why it's so critical for privately held firms to allow for stock ownership opportunities for their key people.

The ability to motivate people is critical to any high performing A/E/P or environmental firm— or one that aspires to be such a company. Stop *giving* and start *offering*, and you may be rewarded with a more motivated staff. **Z**

D E T A I L S

. . . .

STAFF TURN-OFFS: One of the questions I like to ask people who work in A/E/P and environmental firms is: "What turns you off or makes you feel like you don't want to work as hard?"

I get some interesting responses from each of the four main work groups that are present in the typical company. The groups are 1) support staff, 2) designers or technicians, 3) professionals, and 4) principals. Even more interesting is the consistency of the complaints from *within* each group.

Following are some of the most frequently heard turn-offs from each of the four groups:

SUPPORT STAFF:

■ "We don't get any communication or early warning from the professional/technical staff on a big job that will have to be turned around quickly."

■ "We don't have adequate work space."

■ "We get the hand-me-down computers that no one else wants."

DESIGNERS/TECHNICIANS:

■ "There's nowhere to go from here. There's no career path for someone like me."

■ "We don't get pay raises or bonuses that are comparable to what the engineers/architects get."

■ "We are expected to work ungodly hours or go out of town with little or no notice."

PROFESSIONALS:

■ "The principals get all of the rewards."

■ "We don't get any training."

■ "We aren't told how the company is doing."

PRINCIPALS:

■ "That other principal, so-and-so, isn't carrying his/her weight."

■ "I don't know what is expected of me in my role."

■ "So-and-so has a better company car than the rest of us."

Any firm that is worried about demotivating its staff at any level could probably benefit from putting some time and energy into addressing these classic "turn-offs."

■

Valuation formulas

SINCE WE first published the *Valuation Survey of A/E/P & Environmental Consulting Firms* in 1991, we've discovered a surprising number of firms using the survey's Z-Value formula in their buy/sell agreements.

Our feelings about this are mixed. This wasn't the original intention of the Z-Value— a rule-of-thumb valuation formula based on averages for a wide variety of firms studied in the survey.

And if you're selling your firm to an outside buyer or in a dispute with another stockholder or the IRS, no formula is a substitute for a professional business appraiser experienced in working with firms like yours.

However, if you're committed to using a valuation formula, we *do* think the Z-value beats most of the alternatives currently in use.

Our research indicates that 70% of design and environmental consulting firms regularly use some kind of formula to determine stock value.

But many of the valuation formulas we've seen yield arbitrary results. As often as not, they're too *low*, because many are based primarily on book value (assets minus liabilities) and don't take into account the value of the business as a going concern (profitability, return on equity, etc.).

What's different about the Z-Value? Just as the ZWEIG 100 shows national averages for staff and revenue growth, multiplier, chargeability, and so on, the *Valuation Survey* distills 233 different valuations of firms (some of them based on formulas) into averages for five ratios of value:

1. **Value per employee**
2. **Value divided by net revenues**
3. **Value divided by gross profits**
4. **Value divided by backlog**
5. **Value divided by book value**

Essentially, the Z-Value consists of taking a particular firm's number of employees, net revenues, gross profit, backlog, and book value, then multiplying each number by the median figure for that value ratio, adding the five numbers together, and then dividing the sum by five.

There's nothing magic about the formula behind the Z-Value, but it is based on actual valuation trends (other formulas aren't), and the results often turn out to be quite close to what a business appraiser would find.

Of course, no formula can be accurate in every situation. The Z-Value is based on the valuation *norms* and works best in *normal* or near-normal situations. If one or more of the components of the formula is "out of whack" with industry norms, an adjustment may be in order.

Indeed, as more firms have adopted this formula, we've been asked questions about how to deal with special situations. For example, how do you properly apply the Z-Value to a firm that had a loss in the previous year— i.e., profit is a negative number?

In calculating the Value/Gross Profit ratios and the Z-formulas, we have always *omitted* negative numbers. However, to help answer this question, we recently examined a group of firms from the survey that had a negative gross profit and had been valued by an independent accountant or appraiser.

After comparing the actual appraised value to the Z-Value both *with* and *without* the negative profit included, we concluded that the Z-Value comes closer to the appraisal value if the negative gross profit *is* included in the formula. It stands to reason that if you're losing money, your firm's value suffers— that's usually what happens in the stock market.

If you're using the Z-Value in your buy/sell agreement and you show a loss for the year, we recommend that you *include* negative gross profits in your calculations. ∎

D E T A I L S

▪ ▪ ▪ ▪ ▪ ▪ ▪ ▪ ▪ ▪ ▪ ▪ ▪ ▪ ▪ ▪ ▪ ▪ ▪ ▪

WHAT'S YOUR FIRM WORTH?: There's at least a kernel of truth in most old wives' tales. For example, one hears a lot of "rule-of-thumb" business valuation formulas tossed around. One principal may believe an A/E firm is worth five times earnings. Another says that *assets* are the most important thing— he won't pay more than book value.

Our annual *Valuation Survey of A/E/P and Environmental Consulting Firms*, the first edition of which came out in 1991, began in part as a way to test some of these assumptions. The 1994 report examines valuations of more than 200 different privately held firms (none of the firms are identified by name). And over the years we've noticed some clear patterns.

Perhaps the most commonly heard valuation rule-of-thumb in our industry is *half of net revenues.* Interestingly, we find this number is not far off target. The median value to net revenue ratio for all types of firms is 0.46, according to the 1994 report. The highest value to net revenue ratio we saw was 1.59.

The report uses this ratio and four others to establish its own "rule-of-thumb" valuation formula. We prefer this five-part formula as opposed to relying on just one factor, such as revenues.

▪

BUILD VALUE IN A SMALL FIRM: If you are like many principals in an A/E/P or environmental firm that employs 25 people or less, you're probably getting financial advice from your accountant or attorney. Each is probably telling you: "The firm is only worth whatever you can take home each year," or "There's no point to building up equity— it won't be worth anything, and even if it were, you'll just end up giving it away."

This is B.S. The equity in your firm may be the biggest asset you have. The fact is, A/E/P and environmental firms are almost always worth more than their "book" value. The difference between book and *real* value is goodwill. Goodwill builds up by:

1. Growing the business. Volume is the most important variable in determining value. It is certainly more valuable than profits or book value, because every buyer thinks they are smarter than you are, and can make more profit on the volume you are now generating.

2. Getting multiple people to sell work. If you are the only one selling, you will never get full value for the equity in your firm. Buyers will see your company as too risky.

3. Building your systems. This is everything from having a good accounting and billing system to maintaining accurate and up-to-date project files.

4. Specialization. A specialized practice is almost always worth more than a jack-of-all trades practice, or one that is just a "good design firm."

▪

Wanted: Branch office entrepreneurs

THE NUMBER ONE, make-or-break factor in starting and growing a satellite office is the *manager*. So what's the hallmark of a good office manager? We asked some multi-office firm principals recently.

Strong marketing skills. Unless they're running a pure production office, satellite office managers have to be able to sell new work. Dick Combs, CEO at Sink Combs Dethlefs (Denver, CO), a 20-person architectural firm, says a satellite office the company opened in San Jose didn't make it largely because the office manager lacked marketing skills.

"None of the principals wanted to take it on, so we relied on a manager who worked for us in Denver who was from that area," says Combs. "He was technically one of the best employees we've ever had, but he had no real marketing skills. It would've taken sending a principal out there to make it happen."

There are branch offices that survive exclusively on projects sold by other offices. However, few of us can carry this off forever. It's hard to justify the redundant overhead of keeping production offices when the workload declines.

Good leadership qualities. David Evans, president of David Evans & Associates (Portland, OR), a 500-person consulting engineering firm, says part of being a successful manager is knowing how to get people to believe in you. "You've got to be able to get the team behind you," he says. "Good satellite office managers have to convince the staff they can and will make the right decisions for the whole office." The value of entrepreneurial thinking in Evans' firm is evidenced by the fact that all 11 of its satellite office managers own a piece of the firm.

A sense of teamwork. Satellite office managers often say they run their offices like a separate business. But those who don't remember they're part of a larger firm probably won't last too long, either.

"You need someone who's a team player," says Fred Correale, president of Vollmer Associates (New York, NY), a 350-person A/E firm. "The tendency in some branch offices is for the primary concern to be the day-to-day operation of that office. They have to recognize they're part of a team."

Good technical skills. A good satellite office manager needs some level of technical expertise, if only to deal intelligently with clients and get respect from the technical people in the office. "Because we're selling professional services, they have to be technically proficient," says Evans. "Actually, you need to be Clark Kent. But I think technical leadership is part of the role of office manager."

Ron Ballard, president of JMM Operational Services (Denver, CO), a subsidiary of environmental consulting giant **Montgomery Watson** (Pasadena, CA), agrees— to a degree. "They have to know enough to ask good questions and challenge things that don't seem right," says Ballard. "But they don't have to be the best in the office at everything."

Some financial aptitude. We're suspicious of any manager who has no idea of the costs and revenues associated with his or her unit. Even if the invoices and checks originate from headquarters, a manager has to know what makes the numbers work. "From our perspective, we really look for somebody who understands the financial aspects of our business," says Correale. "But you can usually train somebody to deal with finances."

Communications and people skills. A good satellite office manager has to be able to get the firm's message across to clients, motivate office personnel, and maintain a good relationship with a headquarters that may be far away.

"They have to have incredible people skills," says Combs. "That's why you can't always take a person who is a terrific project manager and assume he's going to be able to run an office. He may have wonderful organizational skills and management skills, but that doesn't mean he's going to be able to hustle the way he'll have to."

Entrepreneurial spirit. In a survey on satellite office management conducted in 1994 by Mark Zweig & Associates, more than 70% of headquarters principals said the ability to think like an entrepreneur was the *most* important trait of an office manager. Before you pick an office manager, ask one question: Could this person start and operate his or her own business? If not, you'd better look elsewhere. **Z**

D E T A I L S

. . . .

HOW DO firms deal with salary and cost of living differences when moving an employee from one office to another?

"It's something you have to recognize," says John Urban, president of Edwards & Kelsey, Inc. (Livingston, NJ), a 300-person consulting engineering firm. "When you make these transfers, you've got to make it clear it works both ways."

Duane Roggow, director of human resources at Hansen Lind Meyer, Inc. (Iowa City, IA), a 280-person A/E firm, remembers one young architect who volunteered to move from the firm's Chicago office to its New York City office. His pay was increased 15-20%, says Roggow. But 18 months later, when he requested and was granted a transfer back to Chicago, his pay was adjusted *down* to the level it was when he left.

"You have to balance it a bit," says Roggow. "You can't have somebody of similar quality making $10,000 more than anybody else." Here are some ways firms can approach the dilemma of transferring employees to an area with a different salary scale:

Use an index. Anderson DeBartolo Pan, Inc. (Tucson, AZ), a 300-person A/E firm with satellite offices in San Francisco and Phoenix, adjusts the salary of a transferred employee using an index that identifies differences in cost-of-living, salary, housing and other expenses in certain parts of the country, says Mike Stanley, principal at ADP.

But it may not be wise to rely completely on *cost-of-living* indexes. Just as important are the local *salary scales* in your profession. Roggow recalls when HLM opened its Chicago office in 1977, its principals expected to pay higher salaries to staff in that office. They were wrong. "Because of supply and demand, we could actually hire people for *less*," says Roggow.

Provide other incentives. Sometimes salary isn't the issue. If housing is a problem, maybe the firm can help out in that area. Or a signing or relocation bonus could make a move to a higher cost-of-living area easier to take.

Avoid it. ADP will only transfer high-level employees and only if necessary. Moving someone from Arizona to San Francisco is a problem for ADP, not only because the salaries are higher, but because most people from Arizona aren't used to the cost of things in San Francisco. ADP has never transferred someone from San Francisco to Arizona, because of the lifestyle and salary differences.

Roggow says HLM also prefers to hire someone locally. But he remembers one situation where someone with a certain skill was needed in New York relatively quickly. Instead of hiring someone, the company paid an employee in the Chicago office about $10,000 above market value to make the move. "If you absolutely have to move someone, sometimes you have to pay the freight," says Roggow.

■

What Deming *really* said

O N MONDAY, December 20, 1993, William Edwards Deming, the 93-year-old management guru of worldwide fame, died in his sleep.

A statistician with a doctorate in Physics from Yale, Deming was credited with engineering the rebuilding of Japan's industrial base after the Second World War. He was first sent by the U.S. Census Bureau and later brought back by the Union of Japanese Scientists as a consultant. Deming taught the Japanese how to become the quality leaders of the world, though he was largely ignored in this country until the 1970s.

Deming's "14 Points for Management" are the basis of most Total Quality Management (TQM) programs. Since I have great respect for Deming, but have often criticized TQM and the way it has been implemented in the A/E and environmental industry, I thought we should revisit his "14 Points." After each of Deming's points is my interpretation of how it *should* be applied to our business:

1. **Create a constancy of purpose toward improvement of product and service, with the aim to become competitive and to stay in business, and to provide jobs.** To implement this "point" in an A/E, consulting engineering, or environmental consulting firm, top management must keep employees focused on the firm's primary activity— satisfying clients' needs for professional services. All

other activities are secondary. The mission of the firm must be to fill some need in society as a whole or some segment of society, and to do that, the firm has to first *survive*. Only then can it make profits.

2. **Adopt the new philosophy. We are in a new economic age. Western management must awaken to the challenge, must learn their responsibilities, and take on leadership for change.** Consulting engineers and architects, in particular, should forget a good deal of what they "learned" from their teachers as they came up through the ranks. No matter how much we complain about not making as much as equivalent doctors and lawyers, the fact is too many of us in leadership positions have *already* achieved our career goals. Management's complacency and satisfaction with the current state of affairs is the precursor to death.

3. **Cease dependence on inspection to achieve quality. Eliminate the need for inspection on a mass basis by building in quality.** "Review by a qualified senior professional in each discipline area" is at the cornerstone of any design firm's stated QA/QC policy, although the universal "white lie" for this business is how we tell our clients that we do these reviews and then don't. I have yet to see even once in a written quality policy where a firm states that it will *hire* the right people— those with the education and experience to do the job right the *first* time. And to do the job right the first time, we have to communicate with our clients, other disciplines, and staff. Most firms have a hit-or-miss approach to communications, at best.

4. **End the practice of awarding business on the basis of price tag. Instead, minimize total cost. Move toward a single supplier for any item, on a long-term relationship of loyalty and trust.** Architects, in particular, pay note: the cheapest mechanical/electrical/plumbing consultants will probably not be the best. You are getting the quality of service you pay for! Too many of us think that's

the way it works when we sell ourselves to clients, yet somehow immediately forget it when we are on the buying end.

5. **Improve constantly and forever the system of production and service, to improve quality and productivity, and thus constantly decrease costs.** This is why firms must stop harvesting all of the profits and invest in processes and systems. And that means more than buying computer hardware. It also means hiring the people necessary to operate the computer system, and the additional, high-quality support people needed to get the marketing database organized, the company filing systems set up and maintained, and the hiring process streamlined. And it may mean deciding to put everything on CADD even though it's initially more expensive, or spending more on training.

6. **Institute training on the job.** The training we do provide is on-the-job, but it's not what new engineers, architects and scientists really need. Most engineers who graduated from college in the last five years and are working in consulting engineering firms have never done any drafting. They don't get carted along as observers when their firm is making a marketing presentation. And, they don't get out into the field to see how their plans and specs actually get used to build something. It's no wonder principals are constantly complaining about the lack of skills in those lower in the hierarchy.

7. **Institute leadership. The aim of supervision should be to help people and machines and gadgets do a better job. Supervision of management is in need of overhaul, as well as supervision of production workers.** Management has to be accountable. But again, if you look at the typical design firm, those who run the firm on a daily basis are also those who own the firm and sit on its BOD. To top it off, there usually isn't any kind of scorecard for principals in terms of what each one has sold, how profitable their jobs, departments or offices

---

the way it works when we sell ourselves to clients, yet somehow immediately forget it when we are on the buying end.

5. **Improve constantly and forever the system of production and service, to improve quality and productivity, and thus constantly decrease costs.** This is why firms must stop harvesting all of the profits and invest in processes and systems. And that means more than buying computer hardware. It also means hiring the people necessary to operate the computer system, and the additional, high-quality support people needed to get the marketing database organized, the company filing systems set up and maintained, and the hiring process streamlined. And it may mean deciding to put everything on CADD even though it's initially more expensive, or spending more on training.

6. **Institute training on the job.** The training we do provide is on-the-job, but it's not what new engineers, architects and scientists really need. Most engineers who graduated from college in the last five years and are working in consulting engineering firms have never done any drafting. They don't get carted along as observers when their firm is making a marketing presentation. And, they don't get out into the field to see how their plans and specs actually get used to build something. It's no wonder principals are constantly complaining about the lack of skills in those lower in the hierarchy.

7. **Institute leadership. The aim of supervision should be to help people and machines and gadgets do a better job. Supervision of management is in need of overhaul, as well as supervision of production workers.** Management has to be accountable. But again, if you look at the typical design firm, those who run the firm on a daily basis are also those who own the firm and sit on its BOD. To top it off, there usually isn't any kind of scorecard for principals in terms of what each one has sold, how profitable their jobs, departments or offices

are, or anything else. They don't get performance reviews and they all earn close to the same salary and bonus. And we all hate to supervise people, so we let them go until their performance is so far out of hand it's too late to fix it.

8. **Drive out fear, so that everyone may work effectively for the company.** Principals who must put their seal of approval on every decision, no matter how minor, will have employees who are afraid to make even the smallest decision. When employees are not empowered to make an improvement when they see the chance, quality suffers.

9. **Break down the barriers between departments. People in research, design, sales and production must work as a team, to foresee problems of production and in use that may be encountered with the product or service.** I have been saying for years that multi-discipline teams are the way to go. Look at Chrysler Corporation as an example of how this has been applied in the auto industry. Its profits last year beat GM and Ford combined, and also topped all of the Japanese auto makers. These fantastic results, to a great degree, are being attributed to organization structure.

10. **Eliminate slogans, exhortations, and targets for the work force asking for zero defects and new levels of productivity. Such exhortations only create adversarial relationships, as the bulk of the causes of low quality and low productivity belong to the system and thus lie beyond the power of the work force.** There's no place in an A/E firm for corny motivational posters. Fortunately, not many of us have these hanging in our offices!

11a. Eliminate work standards (quotas) on the factory floor. Substitute leadership. My interpretation of this point and point #11b is that the culture has to reinforce high productivity. You can't force people to do what they don't want to do.

11b. Eliminate management by objective (MBO). Eliminate management by numbers and numerical goals. Substitute leadership. See Point #11a above.

12a. Remove barriers that rob the hourly worker of his right to pride of workmanship. The responsibility of supervisors must be changed from sheer numbers to quality. Everyone needs a chance to shine. Meetings where all members of the project team show others in the office what they have done on a job have a value *far* beyond their cost. Also, think about the pressure we put on the typical manager in an A/E or environmental firm. They are being pushed for higher utilization, higher multipliers, and greater profits. But no one really looks at errors or rework. In fact, many employees will openly joke or comment about how problems are expected and just a normal part of the business.

12b. Remove barriers that rob people in management and engineering of their right to pride of workmanship. This means, "inter alia," abolishment of the annual or merit rating and of management by objective. We don't have too many problems with this one in our business, since we hate doing performance appraisals and often dole out raises across the board. Deming would probably grant two points for our industry on this one (although the human resources managers would have a fit)!

13. Institute a vigorous program of education and self-improvement. We spend a whopping .3 to .4% of net service revenues on training each year in the typical A/E or environmental consulting firm. Yet, the rest of American industry spends *five or more* times as much. We have to learn to invest, not just in computers and office facilities, but also in our people, if we want to establish a competitive advantage.

14. Put everybody in the company to work to accomplish the transformation. The transformation is everybody's job. Again, quality has to be part of the culture. But it cer-

tainly won't be if we cut off everyone but top management from the information stream on how the firm is doing, or if we isolate ourselves in our executive offices. If you really want to get everyone pulling together as a team, stop lunching with your fellow principals and eat with the drafters and secretaries.

If you are really serious about TQM, go back to the basics. Deming's 14 points seemed to work for the Japanese, didn't they? Maybe they can work for you, too. **Z**

What it takes to grow

A FRIEND who has owned his own small design firm for years asked me once what it takes to grow a company in the consulting engineering or architecture business. And although there are many ways to define the word *"growth,"* what I am referring to here is growth in fee volume. In my experience, firms wanting to grow need to do *all* of the following:

1. **You have to do good work so you can keep your clients.** It sounds obvious, but this is critical. Any firm that is serious about growing will have to retain its clients. Getting new clients costs money. Firms that can't retain at least 75-80% of their clients over a five-year period will spend a disproportionate share of their scarce resources on marketing— just to stay the same size.

2. **The owners must want to grow.** A lot of owners *say* they want to grow their firms, but they really don't. It sounds good to employees to say you want to grow, because most motivated people want to work in a firm that wants to grow. Owners who don't want to grow their business are usually not interested in dealing with the problems of growth— things like more personnel problems, a bigger payroll, a greater need to retain cash or take on debt that they will have to sign for personally, and so on. But if the

owners don't want to grow, there's no way the employees can drive them to it.

3. **The employees must want to grow.** Have you ever heard the old expression, "It's like pushing a rope?" That's what it's like trying to lead a firm made up of employees who have no interest in growth. Any firm that wants to grow needs motivated, *hungry* people who are willing to put out in the hopes there will be a reward for their efforts down the line. Management needs to do its part by hiring those people in the first place, reforming or "dehiring" those who aren't oriented toward growth, and creating incentives that make the "growers" want to stay.

4. **The owners must invest in the business.** This means building systems, hiring good support people, and buying whatever equipment you have to in order to keep up with technology. Don't let your short-sighted accountants and attorneys talk you out of growing your business. Most of these people come from small companies where their equity has little or no value. They are influencing too many A/E/P and environmental firm principals (their clients) with their own thinking that the only measure of success for a professional service firm is how much cash the owners can extract from it each year. If that's the way you think, you will never grow your company. Growing companies need to be fed— not starved. Principals cannot be short-sighted by draining too much capital out of the business each year.

5. **The principals have to love working long hours.** You will never get the extra effort out of your people (which you need to grow a company) if the owners don't set the example themselves by working extra hours. Where do you think you get time to develop systems that make the business more efficient, improve quality, or make it easier to sell services consistently? You can't afford to take time away from billable activities because the margins are too slim in this business. It has to come from extra

hours, and principals must lead the charge or no one else will.

6. **You need a good business plan.** My experience is that architects, engineers, and planners hate to plan. They'll do it for their clients, but not for themselves. Why? Deep down they feel it's really more fun to come into the office each day with a new crisis to solve and then succeed in solving it. That's very gratifying for technical people. But growing a company requires planning. You cannot afford to change strategies every couple of years— you have to decide where you ultimately want to end up, and then make sure every decision you make in the interim is consistent with that ultimate objective. It sounds simple, but it rarely is when you have multiple owners, all with different ideas about where the business should go. It's critical that these differences be confronted and resolved, or resources will be wasted changing directions, ultimately crippling the firm's ability to grow. **Z**

D E T A I L S

· · · · · · · · · · · · · · · · · · · ·

FROM ITS inception in 1984, KSBH Architects (Pittsburgh, PA) emphasized technology. But because it jumped into the high-tech arena early, the 13-person firm recently found itself falling behind technology's rapid advance.

KSBH plowed ahead, borrowing $25,000 to upgrade its computer system. "We realized it was time to stop holding our wings in," says Roger Kingsland, a principal of the firm. "If you don't reinvest, it just perpetuates your downfall."

KSBH's risk was a calculated one— when they decided to borrow the money, the firm's principals knew they were close to getting a cash infusion that would shore up its financial foundation. But it still would have been easy to give in to the temptation to postpone the badly needed reinvestment.

Here are some areas where reinvestment is crucial to the growth of your business:

Upgrading technology. Like KSBH, Los Alamos Technical Associates, Inc. (Los Alamos, NM) recently upgraded its computer system. It installed local-area networks (LANs) at its six offices, and a wide-area network (WAN) to connect two of its three largest offices.

"We could always do something else with that money," says Bob Kingsbury, COO/executive vice president of the 300-person environmental consulting firm. "But one of our objectives the past couple of years has been to get the most modern PCs we can in the hands of the people who need them."

Improving work space. When 200-person, consulting engineering firm Crawford, Murphy & Tilly, Inc. (Springfield, IL) completed a job and closed a project office, the firm's principals decided to move the personnel to the nearby regional office. Consequently, the firm needed to add about 3,000 square feet to the 8,000-square-foot existing space. That would accommodate the transfers and the new employees it expects to add in the next few years. The remodeling, completed last month, left plenty of room for the transfers and anticipated hires. It also improved the office atmosphere, and consequently the morale of employees who had been there all along, vice president Steve Moulton says.

Adding key staff. David Wang, president of 80-person E/A firm Frederick Ward Associates, Inc. (Bel Air, MD), says the firm has made a point to locate and add talented people. Not only because the firm's workload has increased, but because he says there's a shortage of qualified, young technical people.

Training staff. Like most environmental consulting firms, Los Alamos Technical Associates was affected by a slow growth rate the last two years. But the firm didn't *stop* training its people, Kingsbury says. "We've had fairly rapid growth this year, so it has loosened up a little bit, and we've started initiating some training on our own."

■

What's in and what's out

WE WORK for a lot of different firms in the A/E and environmental consulting industry. And we talk to a lot of different professionals out there. What's in and what's out these days? Here's what we're hearing:

1. **"In" markets** are air monitoring and modeling; sports and gaming facilities such as casinos and race tracks; roofing, window replacement and building exterior work; rural water systems; solid waste; clean water; and GIS.

2. **"Out" markets** are underground storage tanks (UST); hazardous waste remediation (it has not taken off like everyone expected— projects are stalled, regulators aren't forcing clean-ups, and money is tight); environmental labs, due to overcapacity and resulting price competition; and building structural design.

3. **Architects, as a group, are still "out,"** but corporate work, health care work, and college and university work are the "in" areas for them.

4. **In-house mechanical/electrical/plumbing capabilities** for multi-discipline firms that are primarily civil engineers or architects are "out." They don't make money and have constant personnel problems.

5. **Transportation work is "in,"** but the firms that are all busy right now are wondering what they are going to do when their big projects run out in the next year or two.

6. **Regionally, the mid-Atlantic states, the Midwest, and the Southwest are "in" as the strongest markets.** California is "out" as one of the weakest.

7. **The health care debate is "out."** It's a non-issue since we all provide health insurance for our employees in this industry, anyway.

8. **Management by committee is "out."** Benevolent dictators are "in."

9. **Linking all offices electronically is "in."**

10. **E-Mail and voice mail are "in."** Rude receptionists are "out."

11. **Answering your own phone is "in."** Having a secretary place your outgoing calls is "out."

12. **ESOPs are "in,"** since they are a good way to cash out existing owners on a pre-tax basis.

13. **Professional service firms are "in" with banks**, who are now actively courting firms in this business.

14. **Growth by acquisition is "in,"** with even smaller firms getting into the buying mode. Bargain hunting is "in," but paying too much for a hot firm is "out."

15. **Casual dress for work is "in,"** flashy suits with suspenders and bright red power ties are "out." Flowered ties are "out," rep stripes and small prints are "in." Green suits are "in," blue suits are "out." Brown shoes and briefcases are "in," black shoes and metal briefcases are "out."

16. **It's "in" for local chapters of professional associations to bash their national headquarters.**

17. **Integration of all office technology is "in,"** but CADD used strictly as a production tool is "out."

18. **Metrification is "in" for transportation work**, but "out" most other places.

19. **"Partnering," "corporate re-engineering," and "customer service," as the new management bandwagons, are "in."** "TQM" and "team building" are going "out," as we are hearing and seeing less and less about them.

20. **Part-time Ph.D.s on the payroll are "in."** Full-time QA/QC directors are "out." **Z**

More Management Ideas That Work!

D E T A I L S

HOW TO TELL IF YOU ARE REALLY A DINO-
SAUR: What's in and what's out is
one thing. Fads come and go, and
what's in this year might be out
next, and what's out this year could
come back in again in a few years.
(Perhaps I should have saved my
suspenders and yellow power ties
instead of giving them to The Salva-
tion Army.)

On the other hand, there are
some things that are so far out they
will probably never come back.
When I see a firm where these
things are present, a cold chill runs
up my spine.

Some examples include:

■ Dedicated word processing systems. When I see a firm that is still
using Lanier, CPT, or Wang word
processing equipment, I wonder
how they can still be in business. A
PC acceptable for word processing
can cost as little as $900, and has
the flexibility to do so much more
than a dedicated word processor.

■ Principals are the only ones who
can sell work. This is something I
frequently discover when I get the
chance to work for a firm that has
been on a long downhill slide. Paranoid principals who are fearful of
letting staff interact with clients are
hurting their companies, not helping them.

■ Coffee that you have to pay for.
This is perfectly acceptable if the
company has a vending machine.
But if coffee is made in pots that
people have to pour themselves,
and they are still asked to kick in a
dime or a quarter for every cup
they drink, something is wrong.

This practice is a carry-over from
long ago.

■ Dress codes that require all
women to wear skirts or dresses to
work. Not many self-respecting
women would work in a company
with such an archaic requirement
as this. It's probably illegal on top
of it.

■ Wide open smoking policies.
Sure, when I started my first "real"
job out of grad school, on my first
day I was issued a corporate ash
tray, one of those huge golden
glass jobs that would hold about
two packs worth of cigarette butts.
But companies today that allow
anyone to smoke anywhere they
want to at any time are exposing
themselves to potential liabilities in
the form of disease or illness ostensibly resulting from second hand
smoke inhalation. Fortunately, this
type of firm is a rarity today.

■

242

Work vs. family life

I DON'T think anyone who knows me or reads my stuff is confused about where I stand on at least one subject— how many hours a professional in this business should work each week.

There's just no way you can do it in 40. You probably can't even do it in 50. If, as an architect, engineer, or environmental consultant, you *really* want to be successful, you'll probably need to spend closer to 55 or even 60 hours per week, week in and week out, at work.

The problem is that if you start with 168 total *available* hours in a week, then deduct 55 for work, 5 for commuting (5 round trips of one hour each), and 49 for sleeping (7 hours per night), you've only got 59 hours left. Then if you travel out of town, or work *more* than 55 hours per week, or live *more* than 30 minutes from work, that 59 can easily be whittled down to 30 *or less* hours available each week to do something other than work or sleep. With this kind of schedule, how can you have any kind of personal life (which for most of us means "family life")?

Here are my thoughts:

1. **Talk about your work.** There's nothing worse than the stoic who comes home from the office each day and refuses to talk about what's going on at work with his spouse or the rest of the family. It's downright crazy, and

I can't imagine a more sure-fire recipe for creating a family that won't understand why you work so much.

2. **Get your spouse and other family members out to see the work of your firm.** Excitement is contagious. Maybe if your family sees that you really are doing something worthwhile with all of these hours, they'll better understand why you are doing it. Take Sunday rides out to project sites and explain what's going on or why particular things are being built a certain way.

3. **Sell the benefits of your long hours.** Hopefully, you are working like you are for a reason, to accomplish some goal. The hard work is either paying off already or probably will at some point in the future. Get everyone behind you by explaining what that payoff means to them as individual family members. Don't assume they have the same understanding that you do of what it takes to get ahead in this business. Don't assume they even know what degree of success is *possible* in this business.

4. **Use your free time wisely.** I know lots of people who are successful in their careers but blow it at home. They do it by going golfing every weekend (without their spouse, significant other, or kids), spending every Sunday in front of the T.V. watching sports, going on vacations with their *friends* instead of their *family*, or getting so absorbed in some hobby that virtually all of their free time is consumed by it. If you want to have close relationships with certain people, you have to spend time with them.

5. **Use your *work* time wisely.** Are you really working all of those hours, or are you working 45 and *screwing around* for 10 each week? Too many people in the A/E and environmental consulting business use work as their social gathering spot. As a result, they put in a lot of hours, but have little output to show for it.

6. **Use all of your vacation time each year.** Our own research tells us that most firm principals do not use the vacation time they earn. I used to pride myself in not tak-

ing vacations, too. But I have learned. Take vacations that bring you together, versus those that drive you apart. Instead of Disney World, one of my clients took a trip across the country in a new Saab convertible, camping out with his teenage daughter. Another takes his family to a remote ranch in Idaho every year, a place with no T.V. and very little to do. Last summer, I spent two weeks in a motor home traveling around northern California, something I can attest certainly breeds togetherness!

7. **Don't work at home.** With so little time at home, don't make that worthless to your personal life by working there, too. Work at work, and spend time with your family when you are at home.

8. **Move closer to work.** Why do some people want to live so far from work? Maybe a trade-off from a big house to a smaller one, or a big yard to a postage stamp lot, would be worth it if you had more time with your family. Think about it.

One thing's for sure— this business can consume you. There's always more work to be done. And no matter how successful you are, or how much money you make, you only have so much time. Use it wisely to build a satisfying career *and* a satisfying personal life. They don't have to be mutually exclusive. **Z**

D E T A I L S

RECRUIT THE FAMILY, TOO: How many times has your firm lost a key employment candidate because his or her spouse KO'd the deal? Don't get caught again. Legal limitations prevent us from *asking* candidates about their personal lives, but most will volunteer the salient facts.

Some situations we've observed:

■ A talented planner was being wooed by an E/A/P firm in another state. The planner's husband wasn't worried about giving up his "day job," but was concerned about leaving the amateur opera company with which he had sung for years. Upon learning of the spouse's interest, the hiring firm's CEO made some inquiries at a similar opera company in his city and introduced the man to the right people. The planner accepted the position.

■ A bridge engineer had all but signed on the dotted line to accept a position with a structural engineering firm. There were no apparent obstacles to moving him and his wife the 200 miles to the hiring company's location. He had, however, mentioned several times that his wife grew up in the town where they then lived. And when push came to shove, the engineer's wife refused to move.

■ A civil engineering firm was anxious to recruit and relocate a landfill design engineer whose husband was a bank employee. The firm's human resources manager obtained from her town's Chamber of Commerce a listing of local banks and researched the names of the hiring executives in each one. The engineer and her husband were so

impressed by the gesture, she accepted the position before he began applying for a position in the new town.

■

THERE ARE specific things the firm can do to get the support of its employees' family:

1. *Send information on how the firm and the employee are doing to their home.* Share the internal newsletter with all family members. Ditto for good news or client accolades on a specific employee. What would it be worth to the employee's morale if a copy of a letter from a client with a note from the CEO went out to his or her spouse?

2. *Give rewards that benefit the entire family.* Use food items, restaurant gift certificates, free trips, and other goodies that the family can benefit from, rather than relying strictly on cash.

3. *Pay for spouses to go along.* Some firms have annual retreats where they pay for all spouses to come. The spouses then either sit in on business meetings or attend their own programs. Employees and spouses come together for meals and shared social activities.

4. *Give incentives to move closer to the office.* Provide relocation allowances to employees who move to within a ten minute commute of the office. No matter what those folks who commute 60 miles to work use to rationalize the time they waste daily, short drives make it easier to find "family" time.

■

You *can* reduce benefits without a mutiny

A T ONE TIME or another, most firms have had to reduce employee fringe benefits. But how do you tell your staff they'll be paying more for health insurance benefits, or getting fewer vacation or sick days, without inciting a riot of complaints, grumbling, and defections? It's not easy, but you can soften the blow in a number of ways.

Show people what the competition is doing. If your benefits package is still good by industry or regional standards, make it clear to your employees by providing examples of what other companies offer. Bob D. Campbell & Company (Kansas City, MO), a 19-person consulting engineering firm, recently began requiring its employees to pay 25% of the cost of dependent health insurance. It resulted in some grousing by older employees, says vice president Mark A. Campbell. "But when they started looking around, they realized we still have a very generous plan," says Campbell.

Keep employees apprised of the cost of providing benefits. Communication plays an important role in offsetting negative response from employees. Some firms distribute a list of employee benefits and their corresponding cost to the firm. Any reasonable employee made aware of a huge increase in the firm's cost of providing a benefit would expect to bear some of the burden. Especially if they know the money isn't rolling in.

Trade something in return. If you're forced to take something away, see if there's anything you can offer in return. When Peterson Associates (Charlotte, NC), a 62-person A/E firm, raised its employees' health care deductible to save money on insurance in 1993, it offered two extra holidays that year— the day after Thanksgiving and Christmas— to reward employees for continuing hard work. "We're very sensitive to employee benefits, and as a result, we've kept some long-term employees," says Joseph Jones, the company's treasurer.

Take employees' priorities into account. Some firms maintain "top-shelf" health plans, while continuing to increase the contribution made by employees. It makes sense to find out if your staff wants to keep paying a higher price for the better plan.

Consider a "cafeteria" plan. Sometimes called a Section 125 plan, cafeterias aren't somewhere you eat— they're a way to reduce employees' out-of-pocket costs by allowing them to pay for health care and certain other benefits with pre-tax dollars.

Don't let benefits get out of hand in the first place. Benefits can seem easy to give away when times are good, but they're *never* easy to take back. Fad, Spoofed & Thorn dike, Inc. (Lexington, MA), a 200-person consulting engineering firm, was forced to reduce staff and cut vacation and sick leave in the early 1990s. Once things got better, the firm was able to reinstate some of the vacation leave and considered returning the sick leave policy to its former state.

"When you reduce vacation benefits, it has a negative impact on the staff for sure," says William Gloves, senior vice president at VEST. "You're hitting people directly and it's very, very difficult to mitigate that." **Z**

Zooming in on collections

I N THE past six months, I've had the pleasure of working for three firms with very low average collection periods (ACPs). Average collection period is the average number of days it takes a firm to get paid after it mails its invoice to the client. One of these firms had a 39-day ACP, one a 40-day ACP, and one a 47-day ACP, contrasted with the average for the A/E and environmental consulting industry as a whole of 73 days.

Not surprisingly, these firms were also dealing with their work-in-process (WIP) fairly well. Work-in-process, just like ACP, should be minimized. It is work that has been performed, but not yet billed. I find that a lot of design professionals don't really understand WIP. For example, say someone performs $4000 worth of work on a job in June, but takes until July 15 to bill it. The work would be considered WIP for the time between completion in June until July 15.

What are these firms and others with low ACPs and low WIP doing that everyone else isn't?

1. **They have high-speed billing processes**. To have a "high-speed billing process," your bills have to go out quickly. To do that, you can't be producing multiple drafts for review by everyone under the sun. Nor can you try to do all your bills at the same time each month (we saw that more than once this year). Keep WIP down by billing con-

tinually and by putting out final bills as your first drafts. That way, if a bill needs revising before it goes out, you can do it. If not, it can be mailed right away. An extra bonus is that this practice discourages trivial modifications by overly detail-conscious PMs or PICs.

2. **They have well-designed invoices**. Well-designed invoices are labeled "invoice" at the top. It's amazing how many firms we see sending out "statements" instead of "invoices." Then they wonder why they aren't getting paid! Well-designed invoices are easy to understand. They have a date on them, they have a number, and it's easy to tell what's been done and what the total due from the client is. Poorly designed invoices are confusing, contain lots of excess detail, and make it hard to figure out what has been done and what is owed.

3. **They sign their invoices and always include a name and phone number of who to call in case of a question**. Signing invoices may appear to be in conflict with a "high-speed billing process" but it certainly doesn't have to be. We sign all our bills here. I travel as much or more than any of our readers; yet our bills go out on time, *every* time. Because if the firm doesn't get paid, we won't get paid. That's why I will come in at night, over the weekend, or do whatever it takes to get the bills out. A signed bill is important to your client. It shows that you have looked at it, and if they trust you, they will be less likely to question it. The phone number is fundamental so that if there is a question, you can be reached, instead of having your bill sit until *you* call to check on it.

4. **Previously billed, unpaid invoices are listed on all subsequent invoices**. This, too, is fundamental to getting paid. Firms with low ACPs almost always do this; firms with high ACPs rarely ever do. The reason most companies give for *not* doing this is that their clients complain about it. My response to that one is simple: "Pay on schedule and it will never happen!" If you didn't pay your electric bill, it would show up on your next months' bill.

And I doubt any amount of calling and complaining would get the utility company to change its billing practices! Don't *you* be a push-over for slow-paying clients, either.

5. **They have consistent collection procedures.** Good collection procedures require certain things to happen every time throughout the collection cycle. That means clients routinely get called to be sure an invoice was received and has been processed for payment. That means a copy of any unpaid bill goes back out at 30 days. That means bills not paid in 45 days are followed up with a phone call. It means good records are kept to document all these collection activities. Finally, it means the firm has a limit to how long it is willing to play "banker" for a client that doesn't pay its bills. And it will get nasty (if necessary) to get paid.

6. **They don't keep a lot of cash in the bank.** There's nothing like a little pressure to perform. Getting excess cash out of the business forces you to collect your money. Too much cash in the bank may take the heat off you when it comes to getting paid, and allow ACP and WIP numbers to float upward.

Getting paid is a vital element of good cash management for any A/E/P or environmental firm. *Much* more is within your control than you will ever realize. **Z**

D E T A I L S

. . . .

BAD EXCUSES FOR LACK OF PAYMENT:
Sometimes clients can be miserable. They want you to jump through hoops, you ask "how high?", then make the jump— only to find the client is not going to keep his end of the deal and pay you on time.

Following are some real-life excuses that A/E/P and environmental consulting firms have been given by their clients when trying to collect money owed to them:

■ "I have your check right here in front of me but it hasn't been signed yet."

■ "I hurt my foot." (Go ahead and laugh, but it really happened!)

■ "My wife's father just died and I have to deal with that."

■ "Didn't I send that check already? I know I signed the paperwork."

■ "I can't find a copy of the invoice. Can you send me another one?"

■ "We couldn't figure out what project the invoice was for."

■ "The check came back because we evidently put it in the window envelope backwards."

■ "We're still waiting on you guys to give us the additional information we asked for."

■ "We moved our office and I haven't yet had the time to unpack my boxes."

■ "You'll get your money. But first, let's talk about the next job we want you guys to do for us."

■ "The post office must have lost it."

■ "My assistant is on vacation. We'll get it out to you when she gets back."

■ "I have your check right in front of me. Would you like me to fax you a copy of it?"

■ "What's this $3.86 on November's invoice for 'meals?'"

■ "Those people in corporate... I'm going to have to have a talk with them one of these days."

■ "We'll pay you when we get our financing."

■

Index

A

Accountants, 105-107
Acquisitions
    see Mergers and acquisitions
Appearance, 41-42
Architects
    and business, 53-55, 213-215, 216
    complaints about, 216
    "free-lance" consultants, 56

B

Benefits
    alternatives to traditional, 247-248
    "cafeteria" plans, 248
    flex time, 69
    importance of, in hiring, 68
    quiz, 194
    unusual, 194
Big 6 accounting firms, 22-23
Billing and Collections
    excuses for lack of payment, 252
    getting paid, 54-55
    improving process, 61, 249-251
    speeding up, 151

Bonuses
    as incentive compensation, 119, 191, 192
    based on group/firm performance, 191-192
    frequency of, 192
    versus overtime, 32
    when firm not profitable, 193
Brochures
    examples of poor, 45-47
    importance of, 82
    pointers for better, 48
Business plan, 66
    see also Strategic planning
Buy/sell agreements, 134

C

CADD
    benefits of 3D modeling, 74
    mistakes of pooling, 123
    need for standards, 147
Cafeteria plans
    see Benefits
Change, promoting, 97-99
Chief Financial Officer
    see Financial managers
Client contact software
    benefits of, 36, 147

sharing information with
staff, 141, 172
see also Billing and collections, Financial managers
Financial managers
description of, 105-107
sample job description, 108
versus accountants, 105-107
Firing
see Human resources management
Flex time, 69

G

Growth
how to accomplish, 235-237
in a mature market, 71-73
planning for, 137-139
through acquisition, 240

H

Hiring
see Human resources management, Recruitment
Human resources management
firing staff, 129-131, 153-154
handling complainers, 57-59
improving performance, 118
motivating staff, 96, 217-219
principal "demotivators", 220
smoking policies, 60
staff "demotivators", 220
staff turnover, 132
support staff, 205-207
telephone training, 144
unusual résumés, 44, 132
see also Recruitment

I

Income
see Compensation
Insurance, life, 135
Invoices, 87-88, 250

L

Leadership
accountability, 231-232
and turnarounds, 153-156
as function of management,
210
best forms of, 52
changes in styles, 198
of satellite office manager,
225-226
traits of good, 212
see also Principals
Legal matters
employment law, 60
gripes about lawyers, 136

M

Management
being a good boss, 29-31
dealing with complainers, 57-
59
four functions of, 209-211
improving capabilities, 211
see also Satellite offices
Management consultants
as "insultants", 63-65
selecting, 63-65, 66
Marketing
and TQM, 81
and the firm's capabilities,
149-150
as sequential process, 200
business developers, 142
buzz words, 48
creative, 189
debriefing, 75-77
effective contacts, 149, 199-
200
evolution of, 101-103
improving process, 33-35,
100, 173
myths, 79-82
newsletters, 81
public relations, 34, 100

Recruitment
  and mature markets, 71-72
  as reinvestment, 238
  finding good people, 29
  high achievers, 117-118
  importance of education, 42
  importance of experience, 42
  improving, 129-131
  individual qualifications, 41-43, 44
  family considerations, 246
  to build quality, 184
Reinvestment
  and firm growth, 236, 238
  importance of, 159
Relocation, 190, 228
Research and development, 159
Résumés, 44, 132
Retirement, mandatory, 24, 128
Rules, importance of, 187-188

S

Salary
  see Compensation
Satellite office managers
  entrepreneurship and, 227
  marketing skills, 225
Satellite offices
  buying and selling, 166
  overhead allocation, 91
  managing successful, 89-91, 92
  profitability of, 69
  relations with headquarters, 90-91, 92
  see also Satellite office managers
Selling
  and principals, 242
  sales goals, 199, 200
  secrets of, 202
  versus marketing, 80
  when business is good, 201
  see also Marketing
Service life cycle, 203-204

Sexual harassment, 128
Smoking policies, 60, 242
Strategic planning
  as a function of management, 209-210
  and firm growth, 237
  implementation of, 137-139
  importance of, 137-139
Studios
  see Organization structure
Success
  lessons from Chrysler, 157-160
  pitfalls of, 120
  secrets of, 195-197

T

TQM
  and W. Edwards Deming, 229-234
  impact on marketing, 81
Taxes, 178
Time management, 244
Training
  on-the-job, 231, 233
  reinvestment in firm, 238
Trends, industry, 239-241, 242
Turnarounds, 153-156

V

Valuation
  formulas, 221-223
  rules of thumb, 224

W

Witness, expert, 140
Work ethic
  and "family time", 243-245
  and firm growth, 236-237
  and hiring, 43
Writing
  see Communications

About the author

MARK C. ZWEIG has extensive experience as principal, manager, and consultant in design and environmental consulting firms.

In addition to serving in top management positions at two ENR 500 firms, he has assisted hundreds of firms in the areas of strategic planning, organization restructuring, and turnarounds. Mark Zweig is also the author of the handbook on human resources management that is currently used by hundreds of A/E firms nationwide: *Human Resources Management: The Complete Guidebook for Design Firms.*

Mark Zweig & Associates is a management consulting and publishing firm specializing in the A/E/P and environmental consulting industries worldwide.

The firm publishes a widely followed series of annual surveys on important management issues affecting firms and their principals.

The firm's paid subscription newsletter, *The Zweig Letter,* is a bulletin on trends in design and environmental firm management and is read by principals and managers in firms nationwide.

Specific management consulting services provided by Mark Zweig & Associates include: Management audit; Strategic business planning; Turnarounds; Organization restructuring; Ownership transition planning; Business valuation; Firm mergers, sales, and acquisitions; Information systems; Human resources management; Retained executive search; Outplacement assistance; Market research; Marketing management; and Client perception studies.

For more information contact Mark Zweig & Associates, Inc., One Apple Hill, Box 8325, Natick, MA 01760. TEL (508)651-1559, FAX (508)653-6522.